RELATIONSHIP WORKBOOK FOR COUPLES

Relationship Workbook for Couples

5 Guided Steps to Improve Communication, IncreaseEmotional Intimacy, Reconnect and Rekindle theRomance's Spark

BELINDA BOYD

Simon Boyd

Contents

TABLE OF CONTENTS

CHAPTER 1

CHAPTER 2

CHAPTER 3

CHAPTER 4

CHAPTER 5

CHAPTER 6

CONCLUSION

REFERENCES

Table of Contents

Introduction
The Relationship's Uncertainties
Chapter 1
When Love Fades Through Time
The Unresolved Conflicts
When can anger harm your relationship?
Is the spark gone?

What makes love fade in a long-term relationship? Why does it lose its strength with time?

Signs that the spark is fading

Why do we need the spark? Is it that important for relationships?

Chapter 2
Step 1: Motivate yourself and your partner to improve the relationship

How would I motivate my partner to work together?

But my partner's motivation is low, how can I change that?

How can we stay motivated amid the challenges of our relationship?

The signs that you're not putting adequate effort to rekindle the romance

Takeaway Exercise

Chapter 3

Step 2: Improve Your Communication with Your Partner

What is Nonverbal Communication and Why is it Important in a Relationship?

What is meaningful and healthy communication?

The Art of Listening to Your Spouse

Love is Patient

Communicating Through the Hard Times

Resolving Your Disagreements

How does an open and honest communication benefit a relationship?

When are the best times to give your partner some space?

Other Kinds of Communication That You Need to Know

Verbal Communication

Visual/Optical Communication

Written Communication

Active Listening

Checklist on Improving Communication

Takeaway Exercise

Chapter 4

Step 3: Connect with your partner and build emotional intimacy

What is Emotional Disconnection? How to recognize it?

They no longer share their problems with you

They are starting to lose interest and unmoved from a show of emotions

They are apathetic during conflict or arguments

They avoid spending time with you

They always attend to their own needs first

Why do we lose deep connections? How to get it back and maintain it?

Know your partner and let them know you

How to stay connected during tough times of the relationship?

Encourage your partner

Have a conversation with your partner

Examine how you communicate with your partner and the manner in how you deliver it

Takeaway Exercise

Chapter 5

Step 4: Build an Interdependent Relationship

What is Interdependence?

Why is interdependence healthy in a relationship?

How to build an Interdependent Relationship?

Maintain a sense of self-identity

Keep track of your personal goals.

Be respectful of each other's morals and values.

Be comfortable being apart and together.

Interdependence Vs. Co-dependency.

What is Co-dependency?

What is the difference between Interdependency and Co-dependency?

Why is Co-dependency unhealthy for a relationship?

Takeaway Exercise

Chapter 6

Step 5: Rekindle your Relationship

How to rekindle an extinguished relationship?

Find the right harmony and balance of the relationship.

Maintain physical intimacy with your partner.

Display curiosity in your partner's life.

Be an active presence and listen

Evolve and place the best commitment into the relationship

Use the right words to console your partner

Create a treasure trove of fond memories

Takeaway Exercise

Conclusion

References

Introduction

The Relationship's Uncertainties

Are you and your partner compatible? Do you know each other's love languages? Before marriage, couples first become lovers, friends, and strangers. To cut it short, we don't know who do we end up with. We have little to no information of who that person might be. It could be someone from two blocks away, met through a common friend, eye contact, or characteristics and flaws that make someone lovable. The early stages of the relationships are what I'd like to call the "Getting to Know" stage. Practically, both of you learn one's past experiences, plans, foods he/she hates, late-night calls, and such. The incredible and delightful side of each love story is how it begins.

As time goes by, the relationship stays longer and adjustments were made, as one partner starts to get disturbed continuously by the responsibilities they have to do until it becomes a bother and a bore to them. This is where the problem arises. It can be an indication that one of you is getting tired of the relationship because of the lost passion you thought is fading through time. Our worries lead us to overthink that this isn't going to work anymore and you start to notice the big difference between the two of you.

Your mind will deceive you that you're not meant for each other and it should be put to an end. Just like how confusing the sugar is from salt, that's how it is when it comes to deciding whether to stay or leave. The problem is how would you cope with these challenges with him, remember that this isn't your fight alone. This is how would you handle your insecurities and emotional distress such as feeling unmotivated, puzzled, and overwhelmed.

Is that the main problem? No. Challenges aren't the ones to test the relationship, the relationship itself is. We are unaware of the commitment the relationship requires. We didn't accept our partner as an endgame and calls it an experiment whether or not to end up with them. So when series of hardships come after us, the only option we think of is to end it. We think that this person is not the right one and it isn't meant to be. The concept or relationship is centered on romance, and the short-term happiness it provides.

To ease your confusion about whether or not the spark is fading, Meyerowitz, A. (2020, January 23) along with Lewandowski, G. provided a set of questions to assess if you are in the dog house to analyze if your relationship can be saved or worth saving. These are the questions to ask yourself if you think your relationship has lost its spark and what to do next.

Access to the questions: https://www.redonline.co.uk/health-self/relationships/a30638958/relationship-lost-spark/

After answering the quiz, most of you found out the low connection between your partners or fulfilling results which indicates that your relationship is far from failing. Having poor harmony and communication with your significant other isn't a dead end. You are left with so many options and ways and this book will enable you to encourage yourself and restart to change for the betterment of your relationship. We'll undertake various steps to regain the lost spark by (1) Motivating Each Other to Grow, (2) Improving the Communication with your significant other, (3) Reconnecting and Rebuilding Emotional Intimacy, (4) Establishing a Nurtured Interdependent Relationship, and (5) Rekindling the Romance's Lost Spark. These steps were made to create a stronger and greater bond by delivering simple and realistic takeaway steps that you can follow even just by starting from little to bigger things. Each step is a journey and the footsteps you're about to leave are will serve as the lesson.

Moreover, our goal is to furnish points that are meant for you and your partner to acquire. Before that, the changes must start within you. This book enables you to work on your phase without eyeing the price of the end goal. Every process is what makes an outcome outstanding. It is through a process that we formulate to plan and learn to come up with an impressive outcome. Your development will solely be based on how much you want your relationship to mend, how far you can go for it to be fixed, and how strong is your faith that you can survive and start over again.

Understanding a communication habit is a big factor in every relationship, this is where a man or a woman shows their appreciation, gratefulness, and how to make their partners loved. To accomplish this, we'll start by working with your significant other as a team. As Martin Luther King Jr. once said, couples come on different ships until they live in the same boat. Hence, we still sail on the same deep blue sea which can be a haven or a disastrous area for us. Being teammates means working to achieve something as one. Tallying what your partner did, and how much you've contributed to this team would be a barrier because we're already setting a deadline for someone we reminded to work at their phase.

I and my husband worked as social workers which specialize in helping a failing marriage. We ought to help other people to know themselves and their partners deeply through communicating. We started with the goal of helping other struggling couples and working with them as a team, and now, we have accomplished over 100-weekend workshops and training of different people. We make this teamwork by accepting, learning, and growing through each of our counsel's stories. Behind each couple's unique, interesting love story hides their struggles and hardships they almost gave up on. Each of them had taught us lessons we never think we've learned before. Hearing them talk about their battles bravely had inspired me to write this book, to share how their stories that touch my heart, could also touch that of the viewers. One of the best lessons we've learned is when both partners are committed to change and grow, it expedites positive results and leaves no ground for doubts, anxieties, and selfishness. Instead, it opened doors for a new beginning, perspective, and a fresh start. It is all about rebuilding your faith, trust, communication, and acceptance of each other's identity. Any kind of foundation rooted within improvement can thrive any disastrous waves of life. We strive for other couples to rebuild a deeper and more meaningful relationship like ours, and the result is just as contagious as happiness. This time, we're eager to help pairs all over the world by bringing you this book to apply the following steps for staying in love, keeping the spark alive, and strengthening a long-term relationship.

Chapter 1

When Love Fades Through Time

When being asked what people think when they hear the word "Romance". You'll find numerous answers like enjoyment, pleasure, sex, or other words associated with something regarded as romantic and intimate. Most of us have the stigma of living a normal progression of love. We come to terms for less, therefore, we think we deserve better than that. Often, we want to find a partner, marry, and raise a family. We do not realize that it takes too much to decide too big. Approaching a condition of entering a lifetime commitment without growing beyond its nature allows us to be locked in a cage and restricts ourselves and our partner to grow.

We enable doubts to engulf us which opens doors for uncertainties, suspicions, and distress. The thought of not having the right partner beside us haunts our need to look for someone better. Why? because we think we are consumed and we have given the best part of ourselves to someone who's not worthy at all. This is what our society continues to practice. It has failed to teach us that the person who you are with right now, is the right person. You are attached to him because you found something in him that is also within you. It is never about the externals of someone, falling in love with someone because of their physical appearance brings a shallow foundation to a relationship.

On the other hand, doubts weigh ego which is rooted in lies, and fears. One of these fears is the fear of rejection and engulfment. It is alarming because it may lead us to control, overprotective, and avoidant behavior. It signifies underlying erroneous assumptions like having the mindset of not being enough for someone. We believe that our partner won't commit and stay with us because you won't be as beautiful as when he first laid his eyes on you. We don't see ourselves in them anymore. The excitement dies and we surrender to set ourselves free when in fact, we are always free. Falling in love is not an accidental occurrence. Falling in love is not by our chance. We captivated our beauty in someone else. Therefore, it serves as an opening point to a journey.

Back then, I remember my friend was in a relationship. They were dating for six years. To our friend group, everything about them was almost perfect. They were a couple with a strong bond, admired by many. I often see them studying together at the school library, having dates after exams to relax. I thought they even knew every detail about each other. But when they broke up, many in our friend group was confused about what could've happened to make them split up. We always thought they were living the dream. Little did we know that their spark was slowly fading as time passed due to jobs, other priorities, and most of all, the relationship itself stopped being one of those priorities. They forgot to set their goals and their plans for the future. My friend, Trisha, had so many goals about traveling and exploring before settling down. On the other hand, Paul always wanted to build a family, and he excitedly mentions how many kids he wanted to have with my friend. Confused about what to compromise on, it led to arguments and when ego comes into the mix, it dominated their relationship. It only caused more problems unsolved including problems outside the relationship. This is what leads couples to prefer surrender rather than give up on their pride. Instead of learning to compromise and accept changes, they blame it on other factors like the myth of relationships dying due to a "seven-year itch."

In Trisha and Paul's situation, we can see signs that their relationship was at risk of their spark dying. When they had jobs, they spent less time together and aren't as emotionally active anymore. When I first told Trisha, she questioned me why can't Paul understand that they need to grow up. Shouldn't Paul be happy that Trisha is doing what she loves? I don't think so, because Paul is a very emotional and soft-spoken person. Spending time with your partner doesn't need to involve luxurious or big things. Activities like cuddling, talking about your days, and just being in the same room together will help your relationship grow. Without that time together or connection, anxieties surface as we forget what they feel. We start to pry into things we used to ignore and drag ourselves down, afraid to take a risk because we might suffer and not get anything in return. We should want them to feel inspired whenever we put in the effort, guiding them to the same.

The lack of time together gives rise to dull conversations and small talk. Have you encountered a moment wherein your conversations seem more neutral and logical than friendly? When the exchange of thoughts is blocked by ego, it diminishes our interest to be with that person as the day passes. Inconsistency branches red flags. When a relationship is inconsistent, you often find yourself in a horrible situation. They leave you in an endless loop of frustration and it limits the growth of a relationship. It heeds limitations of what your partners can do. You'll adapt to thinking that your partner has only a little to offer. Sometimes, you'll find yourself wondering if you're not lovable enough, and you're asking for too much. You're not looking in yourself anymore– you're indulging a wave of sadness that shouldn't be even welcomed in your chamber. Don't be afraid to demand too much. Most of the time, the things they branded as "too much" are what you deserve. You are made of love, constrained by love. Therefore, what your soul wants must be declared openly because love is better aware of your value than itself. Speak your heart because it has the power to conform to your bargain.

The Unresolved Conflicts

It is always an element of the journey to experience downfalls in life and relationships make no exception to it. Frequent and sophisticated arguments hold an enormous factor about the standard and longevity of the relationship. There are common catalysts for an individual to feel furious especially when they've come to lose their patience. It lends a lift to the other personal traumas or memories of enraging events. We feel mad because we are being revoked and unfairly treated. We are mad because we desire our partner to appreciates us like they used to and their amount of respect constantly diminishes. It's a natural response to mistreatment and elevated stress levels. People have plenty of ways to precise their anger like crying, shivering, holding a grudge, yelling, etc. within the moment our bodies older our emotions, it triggers our amygdala, a part of our brain that's related to emotions, mainly, fear, anxiety, and anger. which is liable for our aggressive and adverse behavior. The presence of affection is fading when we're upset because our brain is concentrated on releasing our anger. Love compels sensitivity. It must have a vulnerability to one's numbness. Love validates your feelings and holds you in command of your efforts and responsibility for your demeanor at the same time. it's an inevitable part of a relationship to be hurt by someone you're keen on. Oftentimes, we push aside the people closest to us to free ourselves of the inherent burdens of being in love. Still, it doesn't change the very fact that hurting and getting hurt are the painful realities of affection and relationships. It implies that we are caring for somebody and have them look after us reciprocally. It always comes in both ways. Being loving makes our lives lots more significant, and thus, awful and severe.

Relationships often crumble and stay within the downside part most of the time. It's common for couples who were once intimate and never catch a glimpse of every other again. it's common for folks that were once head over heels to reside with madness and hostility, and every party is left to wonder what happened. Many celebrity couples, for example, insult and offend each other, making the media intriguing. It lets us wonder what has separated them. The main aim is not to blame any of us for this disruption. Throwing insults at your partner is a terrible way to justify the breakup without being the perpetrator. This shift far from love often starts with our fear of intimacy, which leads us to act out toward our loved ones. It will begin to convey subtle things like reduced eye contact, lower levels of physical intimacy, a mild aversion to sharing our everyday activities, an increase in doubts and observations, a gradual breakdown in respect for each other's freedoms, and limits sooner. We are always enraged at love itself after we carry out these rituals of indignation toward our partner. It will start to grate on our nerves when our partner looks at us with kind eyes. We don't want them to feel sorry for us or sympathize with us. We want our partners to believe we are self-sufficient and strong. A breakup wouldn't stop us from living our independent lives. We begin to flinch and react as though we are being fended off by these simple acts of kindness, intimacy, and affection. These trends will wreak havoc. As we progress in a relationship, we begin to feel more challenged, and therefore, angrier at being loved. By beginning to alter the dynamics of passion and love with common ways of relating, such as being just regular friends, we can choose to injure our partner's pride or ego.

We can begin to follow a more mundane routine than normal, avoiding the challenging or exciting activities we once shared with our partners. In his novel, Overcome Your Vital Inner Voice, Dr. Robert Firestone introduced the idea of a "Fantasy Bond." The term "fantasy bond" refers to the illusion of attachment we create based on our justifications. It's a relationship in which two couples imagine and live a romantic relationship while maintaining emotional distance because they're normally self-protective while still afraid of being alone. It accepts the importance of having someone with whom to share intimate moments but rejects the idea of taking responsibility in a relationship. When contact breaks down, it's one of the telltale signs that you're in a fantasy bond relationship. You're exhausted from justifying yourself to someone who isn't particularly fond of you. You feel as if you're being encircled and your liberty is being ripped away. On the other hand, indignation is not the big issue here, it's how you handle it. It only becomes a challenge when you can't handle it healthily. Remember that rage elicits our "fight or flight" instincts, which give us the physical strength to protect ourselves in a stressful or frightening situation. It's not necessarily a bad thing to be angry with your partner. It will assist you in expressing your thoughts and allowing negative emotions to wash over you.

When can anger harm your relationship?

Problems emerge when our anger is not fully expressed. It is extremely alarming as it causes significant harm to us and our partner. We all use a variety of psychological justifications to withstand anger, some are considered decent and some are not. When we restrain our emotions to our partners, it bears behaviors that are passive, unusual, and compulsive. Forgetting about our anger and avoiding solving the problem, contributes to emotional manipulation, self-blame, and self-sacrifice. Your confidence diminishes and you'll be allowing yourself to tolerate your partner, which shouldn't be practiced. When it is often observed, your partner can acquire a controlling behavior and extreme obsession. Any relationship that tries to prevent you from nurturing yourself is toxic. It can be a sign of abuse, and because their partners tolerate them, they are easily fooled by the hope that they could change that behavior like some series of love stories. Don't allow yourself to be disrespected and treated with contempt.

It will destroy you physically, and mentally. You will consistently be drained as you feel like you don't have their back. It's contagious to you and your partner's mental health if not resolved and mended. Instead of treating each other with love and care, it is entirely focused on obsession, criticism, overt hostility, and jealousy. You might withdraw from recreations you used to enjoy, neglect your health, and priorities just because you hoped for a change. A person wouldn't change themselves for someone. It is their willingness and eagerness that can push them to change to become a better version of themselves. All you have to offer is your guidance and assistance. Changing someone is akin to entering a game knowing that you will lose.

Is the spark gone?

Falling in love is a wonderful feeling, much more so if the feeling is mutual. You just know that the relationship that you're sharing with your partner is just amazing and won't possibly break or fade. You feel those butterflies or zaps of sheer joy just spending time with them. Even when you're facing difficult phases in your relationship, you just feel that it will last. But what if it doesn't? Is there a point in a relationship that no matter how happy you were, things just get fall off and get boring to you? The feelings fade and you're left wondering to yourself if you still want to continue the relationship. No matter what the situation may be, it's normal to ponder about it or even feel that way. There's a reason behind it, and the only way to work it out is to identify why are you in this current mess, and how it would shape you to feel better about yourself and your relationship, how would you help your partner who's feeling the same way, and what can you do differently if ever that phase were to be encountered in the future? The fact you want to learn how to stop the negative feelings from invading your thoughts is enough of a sign that you want to keep the love alive and help it grow back.

What makes love fade in a long-term relationship? Why does it lose its strength with time?

Every long-term relationship is unique, from the reasons they fell in love in the first place to the future they see and want with each other. There are different reasons why love fades in the relationship, one of these is focusing on how their partners show their affection to them. For example, we, humans, unconsciously set expectations on someone we've helped. We are waiting for something in return. We don't care about the positive effects of helping. We assume that we helped this person, so this person must do something in return to pay back my assistance to them. It goes the same way with love. If our partner ignores us, we'll ignore them too. If they had a bad day, we'll make the worst out of it. If they're busy over something, we'll throw tantrums about the lack of time and attention offered to us. We are focusing on being loved than how much we feel for them. Our love for them depends on the efforts they give to us. That's why most love stories are relevant nowadays because they bring something new to the audience. They normalize doing the first move, and they'll do something to love and take care of that person. They'll act on being worthy of being loved too. Pretty much, all couples have one common goal which is for the relationship to thrive, stay together, and prevent break-ups.

Unfortunately, some relationships don't possess what it needs to last and even if everything currently seems fine and dandy, there's always the chance that one day, the relationship might fade and die. Many reasons could destroy a long- term relationship even without any cheating involved. From dishonesty, doubts, self-hate, insecurity, and even poor communication. If you don't love and believe yourself enough, it will reflect on the love you're giving into the relationship. You may not be aware of this, but you are being consumed. One way to know it is when you feel unmotivated even though you believe that you have everything you need. It seems dull, unexciting, and time-consuming. You lost your will to do certain things that can help you grow. It makes you upset, and undeserved of anything around you. These things can cause a relationship to gradually deteriorate and eventually lead to a relationship, even a long-term one breaking.

The fact is, we are all meant to fall out of love regardless of who we are with at the moment. Finding the right thing won't guarantee your happiness for life because life is not to be like that. Let's just say that you and your partner share a carefree day watching a movie. You find his company soothing, stress-free comforting. Satisfaction drives at the moment and it's just the two of you spending the night peacefully without worrying about tomorrow. The next day, you find yourself worrying about when would you experience that carefree day again amid busy schedules and meetings. But, there's no way or proof to keep the love refreshing. It depends on the neurotransmitter in our brain called dopamine. They are the main reason why our love changes over time. The excitement eventually fades but if you're going to keep the love nurtured, you'll find yourself a reason to stay with your partner and appreciate the progress of your relationship. It depends on how you remain dedicated to your partner.

Signs that the spark is fading

Most relationships go through various phases. But, how do you know if your spark is fading? When you first get into a relationship, your daily life cycle is broken. So, you start to shape it to make some space for them in it. After a while, you start to get used to having them in your life and things calm down. But how do we know if that comfort is just the spark dying down?

Do you prefer to spend your time with friends instead of enjoying the weekend with your partner? This is a hint that your relationship could be twisting down. You started questioning your relationship on whether you deserve to be treated like that. You find that your family gives you more love and attention than your partner. During work, you hardly think of them at all, not giving them updates or what happened. You don't find any excitement in going back home, preferring to be somewhere else than with them. You always try to see any negative meanings or contexts to what they say or do, making you angry or annoyed with them. Planning vacations or date nights with your friends is even more exciting than being stuck in a home with boring company.

You started wishing of building a new life without them. You can sense that you won't be happy if they're around. You imagine things or situations in which you are happy and contented without them. It makes you question what urged you to enter the relationship and what if you don't really love them? Your partner brings the loneliness out of you. Assuming that in their perspective, you're only a shadow and someone to check upon during free time which is unobserved busy schedules. It affects you in all ways possible. You'll constantly feel horrible, isolated, and unpleasant. Who would want to think that someone could make their partners happy and satisfied just by working all day and paying the bills? Physical needs and health are just as equal as mental needs and health. Cancer is as severe as depression. The virus is just as harmful as anxiety and loneliness. Therefore, your responsibilities don't end just because you've provided the essentials. Supporting each other's well-being will always come in both ways. Providing them without feeling obliged shall ensure a stronger and more stable relationship.

1. **The relationship stops being a priority**

It can either be one or both of the partners.

When we're comfortable and happy, it's easy to take what you have for granted. There's a possibility to stop learning and experiencing new things together to a point where you're just a couple in the title. It will only get worse if neither of you is making an effort to doing more exciting things or just simply spending time together and if that habit starts to set in, it's a bad kind of comfortable. One of the main things in a relationship is finding things you have in common and enjoy sharing. When you stop developing any interest together or worse in each other, it indicates that something is already wrong. If anything can come before a date night or spending time together, saying yes to friends and no to your partner, the relationship will suffer each time it happens.

When you look forward to an activity or event that only includes yourself all the time, then your priority is self-centered. Being self-centered in a relationship welcomes a lot of problems openly. Your partner feels they are not as loving and worthwhile as they are to be loved. Your main priority is to fulfill an independent routine. Your focus lies on your tasks of work, pleasure, desire for luxury and all you do is to achieve this goal, forgetting that your relationship is your responsibility. Being passionate about your profession is a good thing, but centering your whole life on achieving success won't give you the satisfaction which will certainly destroy your well-being. Work wholeheartedly, and work for a better future you and your partner both visualize someday. Enjoy every minute you spend with them because investing in a relationship that is grounded by faith will always thrive no matter how challenging the circumstances may be.

It's important to note that spending time apart from your partner isn't normally a sign that your relationship is weakening. It's a sign that you put importance on each other and the relationship itself. You respect their own interest and hobbies, being happy that none of you need to sacrifice their other social relationships or hobbies just to be in the relationship. So, let each other take the time to do things that make them happy and see other people they are close with. It will be one of the main foundations of having an interdependent relationship.

2. **Lack of Communication**

Lack of communication in a relationship leads to overthinking. It would sometimes contribute to you or your partner's insecurity. You refuse to know what's happening in their lives and you simply stop caring about their whereabouts. Communication is an essential part of knowing someone better, no matter how deep the conversation may go, what's important is that you care about their lives, you're curious about their day, which makes the relationship more comfortable and open. For example, asking your partner about that day they had at work if they enjoy the meal at lunch, what are the projects they are busy working on, or did something bad happen in the workplace. Gradually improve until you can talk about deeper topics in life like their phobias, traumas, unforgettable moment, and such. You can also start approaching anything that would lead to a longer conversation like movies, religion, politics, moral values, and even future plans. If the lack of communication persists, the feeling of excitement faded because you decline to learn more or hear their point of view. It can become a risky habit in a relationship especially when hardships and arguments approach us, you may feel that you don't want to talk it out and more willing to let it fester than resolve it. You are losing motivation in flourishing the relationship and if not resolved ahead, it can destroy the relationship sooner.

3. **Insecurity**

Having mutual trust is a crucial step to having a healthy and stable relationship. However, when your insecurity is preventing you from fully trusting your partner, it will act as an obstacle in the relationship. It will make it difficult for you to show weakness, resulting in a limit of the potential emotional intimacy you can have with your partner. That issue of not being able to express your insecurities will put more distance between the both of you and it may come out as other things like annoyance, anger, or disappointment. At the same time, being insecure about your partner's achievement reflects that you're not supportive of their life from the beginning.

All relationship seeks to shape you into something essential you've never realized before. Being appreciative of your partner's achievements in life is vital because it would make them feel that they have someone by their side even if things go downhill. Every relationship is a give and take, no partner will learn how to grow just by receiving everything and failing to put the effort into a relationship where they are part of.

4. **Scorekeeping**

Scorekeeping is overly focusing on the "fairness" aspect of the relationship. It will block your sympathy towards your partner and let bitterness grow in your relationship. It's a biased activity that will emotionally drain both parties. Using it at arguments is an unhealthy or toxic thing to do because you avoid recognizing your partner's feelings or see their view of the situation, you're only looking for holes in their argument to break them down. Relationships are a give-and-take partnership. If you're obsessed with the both of you doing your "fair share" of effort into the relationship, it will only be a matter of time that your relationship will look more like a drawn-out argument than what it could be. Keeping score is critically toxic in every relationship. Avoid listing down of people who did who wrong, who give the most efforts, who spend on date nights, and more. The relationship is never a competition between you and your lover, it is a union between two individuals to grow individually and as a couple. It is meant to help us on how can we make our partners loved like how we love ourselves. It is a give-and-take relationship. During an argument, sometimes when we focused on winning and not solving the problem, it shows that we are not attentive enough to what they are saying. Instead, we try to find their fault and prove our point so we can "win". Humans are born egocentric which means that learning not to be selfish and self-centered takes time and practice like being patient. You have to let go of the burden and obsession with avoiding the blame. Keeping score with your partner's wrongdoings and playing the victim is emotional manipulation. Effective communication doesn't take place. Your spouse doesn't owe you anything for being wrong and making a mistake. Your job is to find a way to resolve it. Don't try to guilt-trip them into something that they're not obliged to do because you are not respecting their boundaries. Avoid keeping the score even in simple things, it lets you devastate your marriage's connection and yourself.

Why do we need the spark? Is it that important for relationships?

What people forget is that at the start of a connection that brings a long-term relationship the spark is always important. Sparks are little fiery particles from the very term, which light up a fire. That spark is the one that lights relationships, its purpose being to keep that fire alive. If it goes out, that spark will light it once again. As long as the spark is alive, it will keep drawing both partners to each other, and keep them together as their feelings develop and grow. After their feelings had time to develop and grow, the spark will come and go. Then, it will be those feelings of love and care that will determine if that fire will grow or go out and the spark reignite or fade completely.

Like any other relationship, there will be ups and downs. It's hard to accept but love is a feeling that comes and goes, and it's up to the spark between you and your partner if that flame will ever re-ignite. But unlike a fire, relationships can grow and improve as they continue to ignite. Hence, the faith and trust that we had put in our partner will determine the sweetness of falling in love the second time. These are some benefits of falling in love again:

1. **Your love will be harder to break**
    As you've learned how to listen without judging, love without expectations, and trust without in-

hibitions, all of the things must fall into their right places including the fate of the relationship. Your bond becomes strong and almost unbreakable. You'll learn the essence of having time apart and together. That's what true love guarantees us, it keeps us safe from the darkness, it helps us to find comfort in uncertainty. At the back of our minds, we feel safe because we have someone to hold on to when everything crumbles, we have a hand to grip onto when we feel like everything is against us. That's the purest kind of love I've known. It serves as an assurance to erase the fear in your heart for a moment because all of these will end soon. There's no problem that any couple won't overcome when they believe that they will be victorious after all the hardships they've shed tears on. Every process is a growth that contributes to your character development. Always seek improvement because no one lives on adapting the same character forever.

2. **Showing your vulnerabilities will be easier.**

In times before when series of challenges hit the bottom rock of our insecurities, we constantly adapt to think that we're not good, and we'll never be enough for someone. We lock our vulnerabilities in the secrecy of the vault, without permitting anyone to enter it. It serves as the dead-end that if someone figured out, our weakness will constantly arise, and we'll be exposed in the way that it tortures our mental health. That's a sign that you need help in rebuilding yourself and the relationship from scratch. Eventually, you'll learn that the scars you were ashamed of are one of the features that add to your beauty. That you are accepted, and there's no way to hide under someone's mask when you are a masterpiece yourself.

3. **Compromising is more accepted.**

As the relationship constantly learns, it is also being nurtured and it sets us from a different kind of approach. It welcomes a new strong foundation that enhances mature settlements when encountering mishaps of life. It's easy for us to express our emotions and even opinions, with the degree of respect that we deserve. When love has a strong bond, the pride perishes in its ambiance. Your thoughts are heard. Your feelings are valid because your partner has learned to accept you the way you are, and they're willing to help you on which aspect you need to improve as well. When pride takes no place in an argument, it's easier for us to settle things and we'll develop a new positive habit of compromising with love and peacefulness.

4. **Improvements will be encouraged as changes.**

This is connected to the previous bullet mentioned. A healthy love will continually strive for developments and it encourages improvements openly. A boy can listen to your problem, but a man listens, sympathize, and acts to offer help. It does not intend to blame and make their partners feel guilty, it aims to support you find your faults, and work your way through them. Focusing only on ourselves never guaranteed us happiness in the first place. Imagine having this lifetime only talking about yourself and not letting your partner interfere with your chores. That will increase the unfairness of the relationship and at the same time, it can promote sadism as well. Choose to be open and honest all the time, even if it hurts. Inflicting pain on another pain causes greater damage to both spouses. Work on your weakness and see it with an attitude of strength.

Chapter 2

Step 1: Motivate yourself and your partner to improve the relationship

The first thing you need to do when you wanted to achieve a goal is to dedicate your time, heart, and effort to it. It also applies to our first step, improving your relationship will depend on how willing are you and your partner to change your ways and habits. Of course, it doesn't come off instantly, as I've said in previous pages, you are both in a progress. Mistakes will be inevitable but that's a part of the improvement. The only reason that must stop you is if the relationship is dangerous and physically abusive. On the brighter side, (Knox & Corte, 2007) concluded that two-thirds of males and females who divorced suggests other couples rethink how both parties will benefit from a separation. They also indicate that it can be better to stay together and find other ways to make the relationship work again. This infers that divorce couples ended up regretting their impulsive decisions in their marriage. They realized that it's too late for things to be fixed and talk upon and let their desire for freedom conquer them. Oftentimes, we expect the romance to stay in the relationship forever when it's impossible. Relationships are meant to be unstable because of how feelings can fluctuate from months to years.

How would I motivate my partner to work together?

First off, we need to admit that the relationship lacks a strong foundation and it needs to be reconstructed again. It needs help and asking for help presents a brave demeanor. Couples who practiced a good communication skill is believed to pay each other's needs. When there's communication, we find ourselves more mindful of how we positively react to their emotions rather than ourselves, they also give the same reaction to us which inhibits a longer conversation. When couples practiced how to motivate each other, they blame their partners less than usual, at the same time, they are also practicing a healthy relationship. Pride will be set aside leaving love, faith, and empathy for your partner. A lot of positive results also come thereafter, imagine a couple who cries with you in the dark and celebrates your success. Wouldn't that be great? If our partner seems unmotivated by what we wanted to do, the best way to support them is by staying on their side. Ask them what's stopping them from changing the course of the relationship. Sometimes, people need a little encouragement for their doubts. Assuring them that the process will be worth it might change their hesitancy. Motivating your partner will reflect how much you've invested in each other and how long are you willing to wait for them.

But my partner's motivation is low, how can I change that?

Embrace the fact that you cannot change your partner's motivational level. The change should be attained involuntarily and must come from within. The most you can do is give him reasons that could encourage him to change. Reach out to your partner by relating to them and how they used to behave before. Show them how that behavior affects you and how would things turn out if they decided to change and adapt to new behavior. Relate how the new behavior will help in maintaining their values in life. However, you should avoid comparisons on how you and your partner cope with adjusting to these new behaviors. This also comes with negative motivation and penalties. Continuously reminding them of their shortcomings will greatly affect them. Let him work at his own time and pace. Let him know the opportunities and future that await. For it to become effective, you should also play your role in appreciating their efforts, encouraging them on the things they can fulfill beyond their limits, and reward them with something unforgettable and memorable to keep.

My friend, Christine also experienced how negative words affected her partner's thinking. Christine currently studies in Law School which indicates that she has less time for herself, and more time for her dreams. Her partner, Reign, is supportive of the law school journey of his beloved girlfriend. He's always there to help her review materials and arrange study cases for tomorrow. When Christine and I had a little chit-chat, she'll always tell me how grateful she is to have Reign by her side. However, due to heavy workloads and tasks, Christine experienced stress and she had no other person to let out these frustrations with but Reign. They argued and Christine had said a couple of negative things to Reign. She never thought how it turned out. It lives in Reign's mind rent-free and he started questioning himself if he's being helpful to his partner or he's being a burden to her. This is the reason why we should be careful in handling our anger management issues. Take care when someone cannot understand what you're doing, always be gentle and reflective. Recall, you cannot take all the hardships in the world. You have a person and you always have to work together to achieve the result that you both want. Don't feel less responsible when you ask for assistance.

How can we stay motivated amid the challenges of our relationship?

To understand what it fully means to be motivated, let's first identity what does it mean when to be unmotivated by something. The root of it all is our brain and nervous system which means that our brain can deceive us into something that we're not even experiencing like the feeling of being unmotivated! Whatever negative feelings our brain may harbor, gets into our emotional spectrum. Therefore, our feelings are based on what environment we live in. Different people affect the way about how we feel in certain situations. For example, a lady just got angry at the vendor who's manipulating her to get her money. As a reaction, you will also get angry at them because someone affected your feelings. You thought that a simple guy, who's working to earn money is just pretending to deceive anyone. That's how it is when it comes to our emotions when we experience positive impressions towards our partner, our activities also reflect that. When we're hurt, we tend to lose perspective and focus of reality, instead, it shifts our focus on the bad stuff that our partners did to us because it sustains the anger and unfairness that we're experiencing. We chose what we feel, it's up to us if we wanted to feel worst, or we wanted to forget and move on. So, the first thing we need to do is to shift our focus to be able to deal with reality. As a starter, here are simple strategies that you can use in keeping yourself motivated while facing tough times with your partner:

1. **Puzzle out your reason.**
    When we are driven by our reason and do everything to make it happen, we become motivated. It's my passion for me when I do things for somebody and know how much my help would mean to them. When writing, I always choose to be motivated by the person around me. I'm doing this for them, and I want to make them feel proud and happy. Simple reasons like that can energize your hardworking soul which could help you climb your way up. When encountering almost break-up situations, I always make sure to find out the reason why I chose this person over anyone else. Why did I choose to take the risk of being with this person? Why am I holding on to them? Simply because they're worth the fight. You'll never enter something if you know you'll lose. You believe and you have faith in him. You'll never bet your heart on loving this person if you didn't see yourself in them. You see yourself spending most of your days creating unforgettable memories with them. It gives you the motivation to keep going because you know that deep down, you'll still have each other at the end of the day, and that's what most important than temporary challenges today. The quality of your life depends

on your attitude. The basis of your future is the attitude of today. Choose on looking at life from a clearer and new perspective. Choose an outlook that you can adapt. Decide on what's the best work for you, and work with your patience. There would be times when everything would crush you down but choose to be brave and insensitive about it. Learn from it but don't let that affect your whole reasoning. It would make you question your worth and existence. Choose your battles wisely as not all battles are worth fighting for. I've learned once from the song entitled "What?" of the boy group, SB19 that even if you start working on something because you thought it can help you grow, you can intend not to finish it. It won't associate you to be branded as a "quitter" because that doesn't mean you're going to stop. It means you have realized that not all things will go your way and that's because our battles can be against us. You can learn how to cry and still be grateful believing that there's a reason behind it. Work at your phase and change your environment into something homey, comforting, and warm.

2. **Recall past significant moment of the relationship.**

When remembering intimate moments, we find ourselves happy and wishing for those times to happen again. It's never too late! Sometimes it helps you to sort out why you fell in love with your partner in the first place. I'm not advising you to live in the past and forget the present, like what I've said in prior chapters, your relationship will change over time as you grow and learn more of each other. However, recollecting special moments in your life boosts your motivation and desire to make that moment happen again, and sometimes it'll help you figure out if it's worth staying or not. It will be a fuel to use as a motivator and create more positive memories while living in the present. When we look back, we see an innocent version of ourselves, curious and excited, which helps us to identify who are we used to be before. Try this method in your partner. Sometimes, innocence makes someone forget all the dark things of someone. When you're angry at your partner, think of them as a baby. Your anger will instantly melt and it'll make you guilty to argue with them. We need to keep something from the past alive to serve as a new reason for our relationships in life. When we've allowed these simple memories to move with us, it creates a new level of union, romance, and intimacy.

3. **Strive for solutions**

We need to acknowledge the problem to be able to seek answers. When we're overwhelmed by series of hardships, we often approach that challenge as an impossible problem to overcome. We've already concluded even though we haven't even tried! But the main thing that we're supposed to do is focus on the problem, what is the problem my partner and I are currently facing? How can we get through it? Is it meant to teach us lessons? How is it supposed to shape us? Asking simple questions like this to yourself can divert your focus and attention in seeking solutions. You'll be surprised at how solutions are revolving around you! It's the same thing as browsing a magazine, watching TV, or reading a book. When we shift our focus on what we don't have rather on what we have, we'll find negative feelings surrounding us and wishing that we're living the same privilege as them. But, when we start focusing on appreciating what we have, it will have a grateful effect and we'll be able to see things from a different perspective! The ultimate answer is to divert your attention in finding the solution rather than being discouraged at how difficult or impossible it is. When we believe that we can do it, our dedication and commitment will drive us through the whole journey with our partner.

4. **Stay attached to your partner.**

Have you ever had a moment wherein you feel like you're detaching from your partner? It's a sign that the relationship lacks communication as you build a stone wall between you and your loved one. The last thing you'd like to do is ignore them forever! For a while, it might be a good option to give the relationship some space to adjust to but as longer time passes on, negative thoughts will pass through the mind which leads you to think if the relationship was worth a second chance. It makes the issues worst, and if you'll both continue to practice that kind of habit, it could weaken your love in the long run. Pushing them out of the picture allows your mind to assume that you're better off without them. It creates a fissure of trust and lines a boundary between you and once it's completely broken, the relationship is on the edge of failing. Once your partner feels lonely, the pain it will cause you can be hard to recover from. In any form and any way, always communicate with your partner. It doesn't have to be an all-day conversation. It can vary in different love languages of someone. It could be an elegant date night, a movie marathon, or simply a cup of coffee. As long as there are efforts, intimacy, and sincerity in everything you do, you'll stay attached to them. The relationship is nurtured, and you'll know more details about them you never knew before.

5. **Your partner is the answer to your uncertainties.**

When counseling couples like us, I'm always fascinated when I ask them why they are still holding on to each other, "She's been there in my dark side." "He's always with me whenever I'm at my worst. He yearned to be proud when seeing me at my best". That's the answer to love. Sometimes, you're just confused and uncertain to keep going. When you're happy seeing them enjoying themselves, that's the reason to keep the love alive. You're already building a life with them the moment you fell in love. How you take care of the household, how you adopt a pet, how he/she witnessed your first job, how you cook for them. It's always the simple things that matter the most. You may be unaware that those little things are not little. It simply matters to you, and the relationship as well. Finding answers to your uncertainties doesn't have to be enormous or monumental enough. The importance and value that it holds answers your question. Focus your energy and attention on your relationship. Restore the love, make your partner the answer to all uncertainties and it will give you a good start to rekindling the spark.

The signs that you're not putting adequate effort to rekindle the romance

Now that we've discussed the different ways to keep motivated during the relationship, there may still be uncertainties left and not most of the time, we're the one who pours our heart and affection to them. If you're like me who's easily hunted by guilt, it's understandable that sometimes our vulnerable side brings out our most sensitive part. One of my counsel, Clarise, is an awesome person which I've met in an event that talks about the love of God for his believers. She has a boyfriend in which is under therapy for a diagnosed case of Bell's Palsy. She just felt like going to the seminar because she couldn't cry in front of him. When I asked why his boyfriend is diagnosed with Bell's Palsy, she immediately blamed herself because she was unaware of the signs her boyfriend, Dustin, was showing. Due to her final examinations, and her part-time job, she's a busy person whose time is revolving around school and work. On the other hand, Dustin took a break from school because of his mental health along with professors who are always absent from the class. Dustin is passionate about his academic career because he wanted to provide a future for them and hopefully move out of their parent's house to live in with Clarise. He also took multiple jobs like working in fast-food chains, coffee shops, and tutoring kindergartens until his body couldn't handle it anymore. Clarise is clueless about the signs Dustin exerts because, on the other hand, Dustin wouldn't let her know about his hardships because he didn't want to be a burden to his girlfriend. When Clarise found out that he quit school and starts going to the doctors for check-ups, she almost lost it. She cried silently at night, praying for a miracle to come through to help his boyfriend recovered.

As much as we want our relationship to be perfect, challenges will always come like an asteroid to test the foundation of every relationship. What happened to Clarise, give her a new perspective that she's failing as a girlfriend. Clarise blamed herself for his boyfriend's unstable mental wellness which leads her to think that he'll be unhappy in the relationship in the future. It takes a lot of sacrifices, patience, and effort to maintain a long-term relationship. Some people experienced a love wherein the spark fades, some is experiencing doubts that maybe they are not enough for their partner and they lack so many things in the relationship. All relationships are meant to take that way because it is a progress of growth. Both partners who are involved in a relationship must know how to engage with each other to be able to learn. Eventually, it will bring out the delightfulness in the relationship as you've accepted that this story is not just about you. You're not just the author of every chapter that fills out the pages because it contains the moments you spend with them. Here are the signs that you're not putting adequate effort to rekindle the romance.

Putting effort into them seems like a bother

It can also be a sign that you're not fully someone who you wanted to be. Loving your partner reflects how you love yourself. If you're exhausted putting effort into the relationship, then there's an underlying problem within you as well. Even though you love them, mornings aren't as great as they used to be. You'll be thinking of other stuff to do rather than spending it with them because you feel exhausted and emotionally drained when you're with them. It makes you feel obliged to do romantic things with them. The pleasure of communication turned into stress when it's supposed to bring happiness and fulfillment. In a celebrity interview, a Filipino couple openly talks about how they started dating, and what are the disadvantages of trying to adjust to working the relationship together. Mikael said that seeing her wife procrastinate and being unproductive, hurt him. It just shows that your partner notices how you learn to be inspired by something. Being productive about your day with loads of emotional and moral support brings out the best in you.

The little things don't feel important anymore.

When you first dated someone, excitement creeps to your heart as you think of strategies to impress them. You think of the best clothes, the romantic restaurant to enjoy dinner, your hair, makeup, etc. All these little things cost you much because you wanted everything to be smooth and perfect. Ask yourself how are these things turning out now? Do you still have the same excitement as the first day? If not, the only reason is that you're not trying to connect and grow with them. You simply do not mind creating new memories with them and that's how a relationship becomes a routine. A tiring routine to be exact. Comprehend how to be grateful for the little things your partner exerts because that little thing can mean too much for them. The same way applies to you, communicate when your partner is being insensitive about something big deal to you. This small action passively contributes to your development that comes with higher value over time. It sometimes shapes our attitude and behavior towards people and the challenges around us. No one started by achieving too many. All things are attained by little things brought together. It makes room for someone to grow, and it makes you appreciative of the beauty that life has to offer.

No one knows your partner better than you and you're satisfied with that

Just because you've been with your partner for 10, 15, 7 years doesn't mean that you know everything about them. Life is an ongoing journey. That's why it spends a lifetime to be able to write a biography of yourself! Don't be too confident of knowing the surface identity of your partner. It does not end there. I still have traumas I've experienced from the past that an experience gave me. You have things you are afraid of as well. You might eliminate some of them but something develops in exchange for it. Understand that everything changes and evolve, our environment, our life, our physical appearance, and many more. Time ripens all things including our growth. You should strive for communication because there will be always something new about them. Ask what song have they discovered today, what are their realizations, or what are the things they wanted to improve or change. A past relationship has taught me that we're bounded to end because we stopped being curious about each other and we let it flow that way. It was mentally abusive and emotionally draining. It reminds me how God tried to save me from losing myself and it's one of the things I'm still grateful for up to now. Never stop learning because life never stops teaching. If you're afraid to move on with the pages and deepen your connection, then there's a high possibility that you're maybe approaching the final chapter.

You Don't Have Date Nights Anymore

I've always mentioned this in the previous chapters. Spending time with your partner doesn't have to be expensive as long as it nurtures the relationship, there's development! If date nights seem non-existent to you, that's a red flag to consider. Your connection is falling into a rut of a day-to-day habit. You're okay with everything as it is. There's no rehabilitation in intimacy and it leads to a lot of couple problems.

You can only nurture the relationship if you're giving and receiving at the same time. Being affectionate and sweet to your partner is enough to make them feel loved. Allot some time to your partner and make sure to check up on them every day. Help them build themselves too. Introduce new hobbies, and explore fun activities at your leisure. Fancy restaurants don't automatically mean date nights. For example, going out on a picnic on weekends while watching the sunset, or reading books with a coffee on the side. Can they hike long trails or footpaths? What are the book genres they prefer to read? Make use of your love language if you can't think of something exciting to discover upon. It strengthens the relationship and at the same time, you'll know more information about your spouse as well.

You find yourself forgetting important dates

Some people are not good at remembering important events of their loved ones but does it take that much effort to make a mental calendar of their birthdays even if they don't directly affect you? Some people grew up in a household where resources are limited and priorities are restricted. I once had a counsel that's being tortured by their maid during his childhood days. He grew up under the guardian of a single parent and her mother had to work hard for them, but life became cruel and they were bankrupt and he was forced to live independently away from his family. Her girlfriend cheated on him right onto his face because he can't provide her with luxury. It contributed to his emotionally defensive side a lot and he still has his share of inevitable traumas and anxiety from the past. He was not able to experience celebrating birthdays as he was forced to work at an early age. He became a successful idol now, and his fan club gifted him 23 cakes for each birthday that he had missed. Your partner might have that same painful experience. Forgetting the occasions that are important to your partner is a sign that you don't value them enough and they don't matter to you. I value birthdays and important dates the most when people forget my birthday or act like it's not my day, I can throw tantrums and cry. You don't have to bring a present with you, just your presence and effort to greet someone could simply mark their day spent well.

You're not respectful as before

Most of us show our best behavior at the early stages of our relationship to avoid leaving them with a poor impression. You might want to work with this in all aspects of your relationship, if you notice that you aren't so considerate as before. Respect plays an enormous role in the relationship. It's necessary to show your partner how respectful you are even when you're not getting along with it. You can convey everything without the fear of being judged because of how your partner respects your viewpoint. You can tell how much you love someone just by looking at how their partners respond to everything they say. It admires your honesty and it seeks to accept. Expressing your interests, opinions, and feelings without the fear of narrow opinion, contradicting perspective, and prideful feedbacks secures the trust, safety, and well-being of the relationship. It also helps you to deal with your partner and other matters patiently and it cultivates trust that can consolidate the relationship.

You find it hard to apologize and say "I love you"

When our minds are clouded by negativities, it prohibits our reasoning to be rational. We are being prideful about our actions even though we are aware that we're at fault too. Most of the relationship that is not fully matured often spends time finding faults at their spouse. It's understandable since you're in the phase of working with your shortcomings and other aspects that needs to be improved. As much as possible, try on applying the 1st step of puzzling out your reason. It serves as a reminder of why are you with your trying to work things out with your partner even in hard times. Comforting words such as "I love you" erase so many doubts, engulfment, and anxieties. It assures us that even though we're in the middle of uncertainties, someone cares about our feelings, and they will stay by our side to hold our hand. Communicating with your partner is the key to maintaining a healthy relationship. When it's difficult for you to say simple affirming words of love, like "I'm sorry", and "I love you" then it already takes arrogance, and no one is brave to move the mountains. The relationship is not as strong as before because no one is willing to open up and be exposed. These words might be two of the hardest things to say but they guarantee haven, comfort, and trust which is essential to a relationship.

Your partner is hesitant about staying

This is the obvious indication that you don't make sufficient effort. Hesitation, whether to leave or remain is the most painful feeling to go through. Your brain will most likely deceive you to leave if you have bad blood with your partner. In a relationship, there's nothing worse than being lonely. This is the result of the lack of communication. Relationships take time and work. Rewards come to those who are committed and dedicated to them. All it takes is time and effort to stand the test of time.

Clarise and Dustin's love and faith for each other made them even stronger now. Clarise held her boyfriend's hand throughout the journey. She focuses on helping her partner to recover rather than letting the guilt took over her. They still have their weakness to work on, but these lovely birds warmly welcome the new challenges that will test the waters. To track your progress in this chapter here's a takeaway exercise to work with your partner:

Takeaway Exercise

Ask the following questions to your partner and exchange answers honestly to determine which aspects of the relationship needs some improvements. Each sentence is worth 1 point, after answering all the categories, calculate the points gathered and find out the progress of rebuilding your relationship with your partner using the criteria below.

Remarks:

1-4 = Keep Going! You still need to work on the relationship.

5-7 = You're almost there! The chapters ahead will help you.

8-10 = Great! The relationship is sailing on the right path. Congratulations on working with each other.

Relationship's sexual stability (10 items)
Why is sex important to you?

- Sex, when done with my partner, is always electrifying and thrilling.
- I am happy when my partner shares the special and intimate experience with me.
- It is my chance to please my partner physically.
- Sex gives me an idea on how my partner feels towards my body.
- It provides romance and stability to the relationship.

- Sex boosts my confidence, knowing that my partner is happy.
- It's normal for couples to have sex.
- Sex is part of a relationship. It's something you cannot always refuse.
- It's one way of making sure he doesn't look for someone else to satisfy his needs.
- I don't want to disappoint my partner.

Relationship's Physical Affection (10 items)

Why is physical affection important in a relationship?

- I enjoy my alone time with him/her.
- I feel the connection through our intimate actions.
- My partner is very attractive and always turns me on.
- Cuddling makes us feel safer and closer.
- You show your love through your affectionate actions.
- Couples are supposed to be affectionate to one another.
- My partner's touch assures me and relieves my anxiety.
- I'm obliged to sustain the physical intimacy needs of my partner.
- My partner will reject my presence and will become cold if I ignored their request.
- My partner expresses his love through physical touch.

Practicing Self-Disclosure in a Relationship (10 items)

Why do you want to be acknowledged by your partner?

- It shows his interest to know more about me.
- Sharing a conversation makes me feel appreciated and heard.
- It lets you know how your partner feels.
- It keeps little conflicts or misunderstandings away.
- I value the openness of my relationships.
- It lets me know why my partner is feeling or acting in a certain way.
- My partner assumes that I want to know his/her feelings.
- Couples should talk about their feelings to allow their love to flourish.
- My partner's feelings and opinions matter.
- I feel more loved after sharing an honest conversation with him.

Being your partner's shoulder to lean on (10 items)

Why is listening to your partner's thoughts and problems important?

- I want to know what my partner is going through so I can help.
- I want to be there for him in the toughest of times.
- I want to be his safe heaven, and that he can always count on me no matter what.

- Making my partner feel supported makes me feel like a responsible partner.
- I feel bad it if someone else is there for him.
- I want my partner to rely on me.
- I am willing to improve my relationship with my partner.
- My partner would do the same if I experience a difficult time.
- My partner will stop blaming or scolding me if I listen to him.
- I don't want to welcome further concussion.

Chapter 3

Step 2: Improve Your Communication with Your Partner

Communication is a vital part to make a relationship work. Through communicating, we are exchanging our thoughts, opinions, and beliefs with our partners. It is also through communication that we know something new about them. Good communication is an essential key to every relationship because it builds a connection wherein it's easier to deal with conflict. The couple talks in a healthy way and respect are observable in between the arguments. It is also the same as important as Non-verbal Communication. Even without speaking, communication can always be there. There can be ways wherein we can express our communication without being aware of it like nodding, body posture, gestures, expressions. As long as it wanted to convey a message, as it indicates how we feel about them. It is communication. When words don't seem to reflect what we wanted to imply, non-verbal communication fills it. I've heard some misconceptions about the saying, "Actions speak louder than words" They don't. They share the same value as they assert both verbal and non-verbal affirmations of communication. How we'll choose to deliver it depends on the love language of each person.

To understand communication better, we need to realize that it works differently in men and women. For example, Mark can be logical and less emotional and he prefers short conversations while Margareth is an outgoing, emotional, and joyful person who prefers talking to someone while watching the sunset. They have their preferences for their partner but they ended up marrying each other anyway. Neither of them is right or wrong because we are simply unique individuals who have different personalities. There is a way to work it out and we just need to find the balance of your relationship. When it comes to budgeting, spending money, monthly payments, and bills, logical thinking usually takes the lead. Mark can be in charge of the budget plan on this one. When it comes to giving advice, listening, motivations and dreams, it's usually up to the emotional one as they know which is the right words can comfort their partner. This is how our body language defines our way of communicating. For Margareth whose love language is quality time, she likes cuddling with Mark while talking about random stuff. There are different ways of identifying your partner's love language such as taking up assessments on the internet, reading articles about the five love languages of Dr. Gary Chapman, or consulting a marriage counselor.

What is Nonverbal Communication and Why is it Important in a Relationship?

Even though there is so much essential advice, counsel, personal experiences on different media that promotes the importance of having communication, it is evident that many couples are having a hard time adapting to these steps and learning from them. They often fail because they forgot to recognize how complex human communication is. It does not only revolve in words, speeches, and sounds, it is also pertinent to learning how to appreciate nonverbal communication as well. Many partners often mistook nonverbal communication as showing your love through body language. But what are the underlying elements that make up this body language? For example, a person who thinks too deep, whose thoughts are always on the trench. Their curiosity about the meaning behind everything can contribute to their frustrations. When they are helpless to disseminate what they intend to say to their partners, they always find themselves be blamed, and we're aware that we cannot help our partners when we also need to be saved. To help them, we must understand things from a broader perspective like body language. Body language is often consistent with warmth, freedom, voice, assurance, environment, time, and patience, failing to comprehend this often results in miscommunication and misunderstanding. It is important in a relationship to know how to deal and work with each other in a deeper sense. Expressing affection verbally and nonverbally has an equal intensity to making a relationship going. After finding out each other's love languages. It's time to work on how can we apply this while keeping the communication active. Now, here are the ways to communicate effectively with your partner and turn meaningless conversations into meaningful and healthy ones:

What is meaningful and healthy communication?

The Art of Listening to Your Spouse

Have you ever noticed yourself already thinking of a response and experiences to share when your company is still talking? To be able to communicate effectively, we need to practice empathetic listening with our spouses. What we tend to do is that we wanted to prove that we went through the same experience but we've handled it worst. People need to prove that their encounter was big enough to belittle other people's experiences which is very wrong. You are meant to help them feel heard and not with, "You should be thankful you only suffered that, during my days"

You are only listening when it's convenient for you. You're not paying attention because you are more concerned about them understanding you. We are all different, what's a big deal for you may be not for them, and what can make you laugh may be insensitive to them.

Empathetic listening is listening with empathy. It doesn't mean that you should automatically agree with everything your spouse is about to utter. We should understand and see why your spouse is feeling that way, what are they trying to tell you, and where is your spouse coming from? Avoid listening to reply. Listen to understand. Listen to communicate. Listen to make them feel that their feeling is valid and heard. When you try to see them from a new perspective, you will understand that your partner approaches another way of dealing with things and hardships. They have the same equal rights, thoughts, and feelings that can help you grow. Listening emphatically helps you to understand your partner on a deeper level. To do this, we need to be more attentive to our spouse's tone of voice. Are they sad? Angry? Don't put any walls to prevent yourself from listening. A nod to show that you understand them is enough. Laying your hands on their arm or leg is enough. If it's time to give your opinions, be sure to view the problem from a different standpoint. Avoid giving biased opinions and selfish suggestions and show interest in what your partner has to say. Show your curiosity and eagerness on how much you wanted to help them.

Love is Patient

Patience brings so much peacefulness to a relationship. It makes the bond healthy, happy, and prosperous. It helps us to communicate softly to convey our message better. It also helps us to restrain ourselves from getting angry or frustrated by expressing our views. Being patient takes a lot of practice and avoids possible abuse and aggressiveness. One of the lessons I've learned throughout the story is the positive effects patience had brought you. You can light up someone else's day when you've learned to master the essence of waiting. It is a calm acceptance that for things to perfectly happen, it requires an amount of time to take its moment in shaping itself. Taking pauses to calm down, relax your rational thinking, and analyzing healthily resolves things. Not everything can be resolved before going to bed, it takes time to cool down and reflect to settle it. You also have to find the right timing in where you're both ready to open up and fixing things. You need to be emotionally and mentally ready to avoid misunderstandings. When you feel that the emotions are rising and taking their tension in the course, take a deep breath and clear your thinking before it could lead to big concussions. We are encouraging a calm interaction so we do not have to take our guards up in a defensive manner. Jon Kabat-Zinn once said that "Patience is a form of wisdom. It demonstrates that we understand and accept the fact that sometimes things must unfold in their own time" We have to wait for God's right timing because it's not early, it's never late, and our faith will determine how much we are worthy of the wait.

Communicating Through the Hard Times

Disagreeing with your partner is never a hard thing to do. Especially when the relationship is prideful and conservative, we tend to attack the person rather than attacking the problem itself. The hardest part is that we don't know if we are disagreeing respectfully and healthily or we are fighting fair. Your opinions matter equally because it is both of your that fulfilled your responsibility in the relationship. When we learn to accept our faults positively, it can be the ground for the stronger foundation of the relationship. When Mark and Margareth were in the early stages of their marriage, Mark always feared how his parents fought during arguments. There was name calling, yelling, verbal and physical abuse, and other horrifying things for the downside life of every couple. Mark hadn't realized that this kind of fair fight was already within his thinking and he's expecting that they would be like them too. To keep the respect of the marriage, he's always mindful of his temper. Instead, he practiced saying, "I need you to leave and give me some space before I say something we will both regret" and that's a way of attaining a healthy argument. When things get out of hand, give them space and practice patience. That statement alone could save many couples from abusive relationships and could increase the amount of respect for each partner. Take a deep breath, don't react, give it time, and think through it first. Ever since Mark and Margareth practiced giving each other time and space, to avoid emotions from overwhelming, and they'll agree to revisit once they've had enough time to think.

Resolving Your Disagreements

Conflicts are inevitable in every relationship. Choosing how can it make the relationship stronger makes the difference. Use your differences to sort out how can your weaknesses compliments each other's strengths. When communications are not being effective with your spouse. Always be aware of the words you're voicing out. Sometimes, when we feel upset and express it in a higher tone, it affects our partner's defense and feedback seriously. It's normal to disagree but your tone and attitude should be respectful to both parties. Try to fit yourself in your partner's shoes and take reflections from that perspective. Give the same amount of respect you wanted to be treated.

Never put your husband in comparison with someone else in a heated argument. An example would be like, "You are a momma's boy, you'll follow everything she'll say", "You are just like your worthless father". That is disrespectful and can cut other boundaries that have been keeping him/her from respecting you. Apply what you've learned in practice your patience and make your spouse explain what he means and why is he feeling that way. Make sure that you are calm, composed, and patient. Think about the issue and your feelings before compromising, and ways on how you can avoid or lessen the impact of arguments like that in the future. When Mark and Margareth started seeing things from each other's perspective. They also learned how to take turns in conversations, listen properly, and it leads them to have an open mind during healthy debates. When both parties find ways on how to improve their weaknesses,

everything good follows. You are willing to forgive and ask for forgiveness. You are accountable for each other's actions and emotions which results in a healthier and stronger relationship.

How does an open and honest communication benefit a relationship?

That ideal expectation of your partner to always know what you want without even having to explain or tell them what it is can give roots to more communication problems. Wishing for your partner to know what you want is like watching an ideal magic show waiting for a miracle to happen. In real life, there's nothing wrong to be giddy and happy when it happens but don't expect for it to come about all the time, much more so when it gets to an argument. Learn that in dealing with reality, you have to communicate with your partner, be open about your concern and express your feelings honestly. Don't go around twisting your words or intention and expect them to catch on. It will make everything easier if you'll provide a room to work through most issues and build a sturdy foundation of open communication that every interdependent relationship needs. One of my counsel's girlfriend had a problem communicating what she wanted or what she felt. His girlfriend grew up being independent as her family was extremely toxic and is very dependent on her. In summary, she grew up keeping all the feelings to herself with no one to talk to. That leads to problems in their relationship insisting that everything's fine when it was not, dodging questions, and getting easily irritated. That's where I told him to put in the effort to slowly make her get used to talking about her problems and own feelings because he wanted her to know that she can lean on her partner, to let her know that she wasn't alone anymore. They started working with it day by day and practiced being comfortable in explaining their feelings to each other. That made their intimacy slowly grew as their relationship progressed and through patience, she continuously improved over time. Sometimes, the childhood environment of your partner also plays a role in developing their character today. One of the reasons why you should be gentle in helping your partner is because they have a bad experience in their childhood phase that's waiting to be solved until now. Giving them time and space will bring a comforting aura to the relationship which can heal the wound of the past.

When are the best times to give your partner some space?

Knowing when to or not to communicate also plays a role in taking effective communication. It is best to assist your partner in distress by allowing him time to distort his work and home problems when your partner is recently involved in a stressful event. Stress can significantly influence the way the communication will be produced, and we can expect both parties to experience a negative result. When you come to your home from work, make sure that you have a lot of work to do. After being stressed, we all want to have some relaxing thing to do. There is no benefit from adding more stress to what you and your partner are already experiencing. It is also best to give your partner some space especially if he is not in the mood to talk. We all have a share of our good and worst days. During those bad days, it would be important if we can avoid harmful conversations and accept that it may not be the best time to explain ourselves about important issues. However, do not use this as an excuse to forget the argument that needs to be resolved. The earlier you resolve them, the more beneficial it will be to you and your partner. Set some time aside to talk things out. Lastly, give yourself and your partner some space when everything is in a rush. We forget about the importance of communication when we have some other significant things to do. When we're in a rush, we are not patient with what our partners wanted to say and we are not attentive to how can we respond respectfully. We're not listening because we're occupied with settling things so we could leave. If you're busy, say so. If you think that it's not the best time to discuss matters, say so. Communicate openly and honestly with your partner because that's the only way to avoid confusion, misunderstandings, and being prideful. Don't assume that your partner knows everything you expect him to know. The only way to heal is to clarify things, say what you feel, listen properly, and work together to get through it. Respectful Communication is the key to a successful relationship.

Other Kinds of Communication That You Need to Know

As we keep saying in this book, communication is the main key in revitalizing one's relationship. But what kind of communication are we talking about? We're talking about every way of communication you can do because making relationships grow is both simple and complex. Building it is a process in itself and the practice of communication bridges the gap and makes it overall easier on both of you. For example, when you learn that you have something in common with your partner. You'll feel more connected with them. In turn, you'll be able to listen better and be more willing to support or help them towards their goals. Another thing on why communication is important because it builds empathy towards your partner. Empathy is being able to look at situations from another's perspective. It allows us to understand and relate with others, may it be celebrating their success or be there when they're down. That's why it's essential because it allows both partners to take a step back and look at the problem/fight from the other's viewpoint. It will be easier to move past mistakes and decide to compromise for both partners. If the relationship lacks empathy, simply put, they will slowly start to not care about the other or the relationship itself. That's why communication is important in any relationship, especially if you're in a long-distance one. It allows you to explain yourself to someone else what you want or need in the relationship, and also allows you to listen and understand your partner's wants or need, making it easier for both of you to find compromises with each other and help each other grow and improve rather than outright changing each other. Understanding how you communicate is the first step to communicate more effectively with your partner. So, we'll explore these 5 ways of communication.

Verbal Communication

We all know that this is the most common way of communication, especially during these times of pandemic. It can be face-to-face, over the phone, or more recently through various social media messaging applications. We all know it uses language as a sentence or bits of dialogue but there are unique cues that others dismiss like any words or phrases can be misunderstood. It depends on the level and complexity of those words, how we use those two factors to give our message. The level of your words is about how fluent you are with the language, meaning how easily you can find words in that language to accurately express yourself. It also includes how knowledgeable you are about the language's phonetic rules, spelling, syntax, grammar, and pronunciation. If you think about what and how will you say it, you can avoid those words from being misunderstood. It can also give your words more weight and connect to your partner more positively. It will slowly lead to more happy interactions that will improve both trust and communication in the relationship.

Visual/Optical Communication

Eye contact is the purest form of communication. It displays a depth of emotions our words couldn't express. A person can tell us a lie and we can become aware of it by how their eyes communicate with us. Before we even had language, we communicate through visual and optical cues like symbols and stone carvings. It's more apparent in modern times as we use images or videos to convey a message. For example, we use emojis in messaging and social media to express our thoughts. Those emojis are there to communicate things that aren't easily expressed like feelings or reactions. Another example would be people themselves liking their hairstyle, tattoos, and facial expressions. It gives you that first impression of what the person could be like and you use that impression if you have similar interests with them that make you want to communicate with them more.

Written Communication

Whether it's for work, studies, relationships, or even just your hobbies, written communication is and always will be a medium to convey information and express your feelings in a more precise and concise way. Because when we're overflowing with emotion, we sometimes find it hard to face our feelings or forget how to express them. There's also something special with written communication than just an easier way of communicating. It's also a way to look deeper into a person's personality because by writing long letters, we get to see deeper and more complex thoughts that texting couldn't do. Instead of only reading it through a screen, you can get to hold and feel the message they want to give. For example, love letters and poems. Sending one to your partner means you dedicated your time to them and want to connect with them. Even though your grammar or structure is bad, it can still make them feel loved and appreciated and give a deeper sense of intimacy in the relationship.

Active Listening

In my viewpoint, this is commonly unnoticed but very important in communication. If we aren't actively listening to someone, we can't engage or connect with them at all. For Example, you're currently talking with your partner about something bad that recently happened. You said something along the lines of "My cat just died." and they replied with "Yeah, that happens." How would that make you feel? You shared a vulnerable moment and they didn't even try to react. You wanted them to at least show some sympathy. That's why in my opinion, active listening is another type of communication. It allows you both to know what you should do and what your partner wants and needs, making it easier to have a fulfilling relationship.

Now, we have widened our approach and views about communication in a relationship. So, I'll leave you with a hint or a "too long didn't read" of sorts. Just speak truly to your partner with expressions. Don't hide, and just trust them. There's no point in bringing in doubt or anxiety when you can try to understand both your partner's and your side first. Practice being vulnerable but also be watchful for cues on how your partner reacts and listens to you. Realize now that no one is perfect, so it's important to acknowledge when you've done a mistake and call out your partner when they're doing a mistake. Help them realize that it is necessary to keep communication strong and true.

Checklist on Improving Communication

Here's a checklist of things you should do when interacting with your partner as a starting point on what to focus on:

- *Set aside time to talk. That means no distractions like computers or TVs and talking with other people on the phone.*
- *Take some time to think about what you want to say.*
- *Be precise on what you want to talk about*
- *Express your message clearly. Don't be mad if you need to repeat it. Watch your tone and how you say it.*
- *Talk about what happened and how it made you feel. Accept responsibility for those feelings.*
- *Talk about your wants or needs.*
- *Listen to your partner. Put down your own beliefs for now and try to see things from their point of view - how they feel, what they want or need.*
- *Compromise and remember that you don't have to be in the right every time. If it's something trivial, accept what happened and move on.*

Takeaway Exercise

Ask the following interactive questions to your partner and exchange answers to determine whether you're making progress in building emotional intimacy with them and which aspects need some improvements.

1. What's one thing you wish you could do on a perfect day?
2. Is there a worthy memory that makes you reminisce about your childhood? What is it?
3. How do you express your emotional reaction when dealing with hardships?
4. What's the best thing about being in a relationship with me?
5. If you can describe your past experiences in a movie or a book, what would it be?
6. What's a weird trait or personality of yourself that you would like to fix?
7. When do you feel most appreciated?
8. If we were to spend a vacation somewhere, where would you like to bring me?
9. What are the five things that you are most thankful for right now?
10. How many kids would you like our family to have?

Chapter 4

Step 3: Connect with your partner and build emotional intimacy

Our partners are the ones with whom we feel most at ease. It's incredible to have someone with whom you can be completely truthful and transparent about everything, particularly when those feelings are mutual. It's comforting to know that someone will always be there for you. That's why it's so painful to watch your partner drift apart. Differences begin to emerge, and you notice that your partner is losing the same amount of love and affection as you are. It's one of the most perplexing and frightening periods of a relationship. You begin to feel alone, and anxiety sets in, eroding your partner's confidence, comfort, and intimacy. As time passes, the sense of loneliness will expand, as will the distance between you and your partner. The feeling can be interpreted as a warning that something needs to be taken care of. Talking about it, and taking the initiative to do so, would greatly benefit your wellbeing and the health of your relationship. You deserve a romantic relationship that grows closer and more intimate as time passes, benefiting both you and your partner.

What is Emotional Disconnection? How to recognize it?

Emotional Disconnection is a stage in a relationship where one or both partners don't feel the same degree of intimacy as they did earlier in the relationship. As you grow farther apart rather than closer together, the feeling of shared openness of love has faded. Since you and your partner are rarely on the same emotional page, you will have more problems as anxiety sets in, and you will lose confidence and comfort in your partner. It also doesn't help that the process is always sluggish. When contact or quality time declines, it's an indication that something isn't quite right. The explanation could be as simple as a misunderstanding or a dramatic shift in quality time, or it could be more serious, such as a betrayal. But, whatever the cause, you should try to find out what the primary reason is. Begin to ponder: when did it first appear? What had happened previous to that? What should I do about it? Getting a general understanding of the problem's condition is the first step in deciding where to look and what to do next.

You must also recognize that, in some cases, having an emotional distance from your partner is not necessarily a bad thing. Your current relationship could be unhealthy or even dishonest, and your emotional disconnection is a warning that you should rethink what you have. Are they assisting you in being a better person? Or are they the one who is preventing you from moving forward? When you're in trouble, who would come to your aid? Is it true that they're the ones who got you into this mess in the first place? That's why you should analyze it critically, considering not only what's best for your partner, but also what's best for you and the relationship as a whole. Emotional Disconnection is common in relationships and will occur at some point. In this case, it's a red flag that something has to be done about it. To help you understand how to identify mental disconnection and how to overcome it. Here are a few warning signs as well as few stories from past consulting experiences when counseling in various situations as well as some takeaways through their journey of acceptance.

They no longer share their problems with you

When you're in a relationship, your partner is the one person you can and should always trust. It is because of them that you have someone to turn to while you are dealing with personal issues. You should still talk about your problems to find consolation or answers. If you find that your partner is addressing their concerns and problems on their own, and they are no longer looking forward to getting your assistance when they are stressed or bothered by something, this is a red flag. They will occasionally discuss it, but if you try to ask them questions or probe further into the issue, they will not respond. If they share it with others, it becomes much more of a sign and a concern. When Mary and Carlo first got married, they always make sure to consult each other whenever making a decision. When Mary faced a problem regarding her work environment, Carlo doesn't seem to notice it as Mary continues living normally. Even if it doesn't involve your partner, you should always make sure to tell them what's going on with your life. Thinking that they won't be much of help is simply putting a barrier between you and them. Your partner's responsibility is to listen to your difficulties to alleviate your worries and anxieties. Nonetheless, the reason why you decided to enter a relationship is to share your burden, happiness, and loneliness with someone. Enable yourself to be comfortable in exposing your shortcomings.

They are starting to lose interest and unmoved from a show of emotions

It's a usual conversation that you and your partner have almost every day about how their day has gone.

However, you begin to find that your partner is easily distracted when you interact with them. Instead of actively engaging in the discussion, they demonstrate a lack of interest when you say a story about something interesting that happened during your day. If you try to talk to them about your personal feelings or issues that are starting to bother you, they don't seem to care about what you have to say or how you feel. It doesn't impress them in the least when you're upset, welling up, or crying. It's as if the sense of intimacy you once shared with them has vanished. Mary and Carlo's discussions are becoming formal and brief rather than informal as they continue to keep their matters confidential. They don't ask each other how their days went very much, which leads to the conclusion that one of them is keeping a lot of secrets from the other. They're becoming suspicious of each other and the trust is consequently decaying. Your problems seem to weigh you down stronger than before and all you can do is cry silently at night. You are locking yourself up without giving anyone permission to enter and help you. When allowing yourself to be weak, crying out your frustrations in front of them doesn't make you less strong. It displays braveness as you accepted that you're not perfect and bad days would be inevitable for you.

They are apathetic during conflict or arguments

Most relationships clash and quarrel most of the time. But it's terrible when it happens and the partner refuses to sort things out or talk about it. When you're the only one who wanted to work it out so that you can both fix your errors, step forward, and improve. However, if your partner is uninterested in talking things out with you and doesn't seem to mind if the issues stay unresolved, you should be worried. They show no emotion, which causes them to be uninterested in your explanations or to simply leave and walk away. When you try to convince them to talk it out, they can become irritated or angry, leaving you with no space or say in the situation. Mary had then started giving little concerns whenever they had heated arguments and fights. She finds Carlo annoying and wishes that she never dated him. "It's just so frustrating when someone you thought is going to be there for you, will be the first to leave you hanging" Mary continuously regrets having Carlo in her life. Mary expected Carlo to know that she's not okay and that he would comfort her. As a way of revenge, Mary would ignore her husband during weekends to party with her friends. She wanted to use this routine as an excuse for a divorce attempt. This is what happens when we decline to open up doors for someone close to us. Rejecting to seek help creates more hardships in a relationship. That's why when we fail to understand that we need help, we're detracting the blame to someone whom we expected to reach us out.

They avoid spending time with you

Your partner, as with many other partnerships, is the one with whom you'll spend the majority of your time. So, naturally, spending time with them should be one of the most enjoyable and exciting aspects of your activities. It doesn't have to be something expensive, such as a trip to the park or the beach. You simply enjoy being in their company, even if you're doing nothing at all. When you're emotionally estranged, though, they begin to stop making plans with you or find a reason not to invite you to do something together. They ignore you or claim to be busy doing something else instead of referring to how much they enjoy your company. You caught them making excuses to avoid being with you when you asked them out on a date night. Ask a few questions as to why your partner chose to spend less time than normal. Determine whether they need space or time away from you. You can be unaware of your partner's emotional and mental struggles at times. Tell them in such a way that they won't feel obligated to tell you. Assist them in getting through it because most people wanted to be busy to avoid feeling a negative emotion. When addressing them, always choose to be gentle and compassionate.

They always attend to their own needs first

Love is never selfish and self-centered. When people fall into the negative part of the relationship, they are prone to think emotionally rather than being rational. As a result, they are often more favorable to themselves than to their partner. They feel that they are always right and their partners must apprehend their shortcomings. During arguments, it's inevitable to keep yourself from discussing the efforts you've both made. When Mary was in the same situation, she'll always think that if it weren't for her, Mark would be homeless by now. We are focused on the ugly parts of something and we are focusing our energy on making them feel bad. Check up on yourself, "Does doing these things will make the situation better?" You'll still be sad at the end of the day, wondering how did all become wrong. It's the fault of both parties, they insisted that they can handle problems without telling the other one. As a consequence, they should show that they are strong which hinders them from giving affection to their partners. Always keep in mind that both of you invested their time and efforts into building this relationship. Help your partner be nurtured and seek to be nurtured by them. You can't deny forever that you need to feel loved and give love to people especially the ones who hold a special place in your heart.

Why do we lose deep connections? How to get it back and maintain it?

The reasons for the breakup of the link can range from personal problems to issues in the relationship. Although the most common cause is a lack of communication and understanding between you, it can easily be complicated by other factors such as work, anxieties, insecurities, and so on. Emotional Disconnection is never a self-resolving problem. The longer you wait to talk about or resolve this problem, the more severe the disconnect will become and the more difficult it will be for both of you. It depends on what existed before the negative changes in the relationships, and determining what went wrong is the first step toward regaining that close intimacy. Fixing the link takes a lot of time, and to be frank, some of your attempts can fail and backfire. As a consequence, you'll need patience and perseverance. They can be taken aback at first when you ask these unexpected questions. However, after some time, they will warm up to you and understand that this is an issue that must be addressed. It does not only require your effort, but also that of your partner. You are still in this relationship, and if only one of you can work on it, things will never get better. Deepen the understanding of your partner beyond what you already learned. You don't have to wait for them to open up before telling them what's wrong, what their problems are, and what they want to do about it. Listen to your partner and find out what they want to do, then suggest what you want to do as well. If your interests clash, find a middle ground or a compromise and continue from there. These are some suggestions that I always give to my counsels who are having relationship problems. They don't act just like a simple step to help you reconnect with your partner; they also serve as a guide to help you improve your partner's closeness or intimacy in general. They are easy steps that everyone can understand and comprehend, but they are far more difficult to put into practice and make a habit of.

Know your partner and let them know you

Think about it. How well do you know your significant other? You're probably aware of how your partner behaves during an argument, right? But do you know why your partner behaves the way he or she does? What about the languages of love? The things or actions that make your partner feel the most love or affection are known as love languages. The most popular love language, for example, is Quality Time. Even if you think you know everything there is to know about your partner, the good part about being in a relationship is that you never stop learning new stuff about each other. It may be anything as simple as discovering they despise soggy cereal, or something more significant like learning about a hidden dream they have, such as baking or teaching. When Hannah and Justin were in the beginning phase of their relationship, Hannah hated Justin for playing games and dividing his attention on the screen and to what she's saying. On the other hand, Justin believes that there's time allotted for being affectionate because his love language is physical touch. When having conflicting love languages, it would be best to know each other, to find ways how can you resolve and adjust to each other's needed. Some tidbits of knowledge about them would be exciting to come across. Intimacy is characterized as a near bond and confidence. It includes sharing information that you won't be able to share with someone else, as well as something very personal. Many years into your relationship, and even after marriage, the process of improving your connection will continue.

1. **Attention**

    Make sure you have your partner's full attention when interacting with them. This means you shouldn't believe your partner is paying attention only because you're speaking. Instead, ask yourself if this is a good time and place to talk about private matters. Especially if it's something important to you or your relationship. If you're listening and your partner starts talking when concentrating on something, take your time to say that you're distracted by something. Hannah wants Justin's undivided attention whenever she's sharing something because that's her way to feel heard and valid. She opened up to her partner about this, and they're able to come upon an agreement to put each other's business aside when someone's talking like turning off their phones, pausing the game, and listening attentively to what they wanted to convey. When partners are communicating effectively, it gives root to many solutions, alternatives, and agreement which makes the bond stronger. Ask your partner if you can accomplish it first before discussing things with you. Giving your undivided attention will make them feel understood, heard, and loved. It is a simple gesture but it would impact the communication greatly. If you make a promise like this but forgot to act on it, your partner will most likely lose faith in you. It's important to remember that both the speaker and the listener have a role to play in keeping the dialogue clean and clear.

2. **Language**

The main issue with arguing is that the other person thinks their point of view is right. That may seem self-evident, but the way you attempt to articulate your point will have a huge impact on your partner's reaction, particularly if you express it negatively. Assume you and your wife have been arguing over household duties, and your partner begins to scream at you, accusing you of never taking out the garbage or washing the dishes. You could not have paid attention to what she said and just concentrated on their sound rather than their actual message. Their tone insulted you which made you defensive of yourself until a part of your thinking convinces you that your wife is at fault. It makes you feel personally attacked, with the tone suggesting that you are lazy and unhelpful, and once emotions enter the picture, both of you are likely to feel sour, finding the blame even if it costs a fortune. Communication is all about the language; no matter how careful you are about your wording or tone, misunderstandings can occur. Don't punish your partner if they misunderstood your words and then discover you meant something completely different. You can try to justify yourself, but don't go any further. Allow the moment to move forward and forgive; bringing it up again would just trigger more issues and may damage the relationship in the long run. There will be moments where what you say or do is misunderstood, and it's okay to be upset if your partner doesn't get it. The best you can do is to prevent them from evolving into anything bigger; misunderstandings are supposed to be swept under the rug because they're just honest mistakes and neither of you should be held accountable for that.

3. **Compromising**

Ask yourself. Have there been times where you interrupted your spouse and then said your point of view, or used your partner's flaws or mistakes to get back at them? It's not only rude and impolite but it slowly forms an obstacle to grow mutual respect and understanding. We already know that everyone has flaws, and your partner is not an exception. If you choose to focus on your partner's mistakes, your relationship is bound to go down. To further grow your relationship, you can choose to compromise and tell them that it's okay to make mistakes. Instead of pointing out what went wrong, you can tell them what they can improve on. When you're not focusing on all the ways that your partner doesn't live up to your romantic ideal, you give yourself the room to appreciate all the things that make your partner great and you can love them for who they are.

Also, compromising for your partner doesn't mean you're giving in to demand. It doesn't mean that you've lost the argument. To be honest, it's the opposite. It's just so hard to compromise, much more so if you think you're in the right. Compromising means that you commit to your relationship because to you, it's something more important than your ego and insecurities.

Even if you want the argument to end that way because it makes sense to you and your partner's suggestion is far from it. Take it from their side of view and look at the argument objectively. What's the logical solution for the argument? If it's something trivial, even if you're in the right, there's no harm in letting it slide for now. Wait for the both of you to calm down, and then talk about it. The important thing is not getting your way, it's staying in the relationship and helping it grow.

4. **Give it time**

When you spend time apart, it can intensify your longing for each other as a result of needing to embrace when the time comes. It's a good sign that you'll still have time for yourself. In a relationship, self-love should be maintained. It keeps the relationship fresh by allowing you and your partner to maintain their identities and individuality while still becoming a couple. It also encourages self-sufficiency and strength rather than dependency and clinginess. You also have the freedom to follow your passions and the time to learn more about yourself. It's a healthy way to stop suffocating each other with the fact that you have to spend the whole day with your partner. You'll be happier if your partner allows you to engage in the new events you've planned for the day while supporting your desire to seek new experiences individually and with them.

How to stay connected during tough times of the relationship?

Reconnection efforts can necessitate patience and perseverance. You make attempts to reconnect, only to have them backfire. You and your partner may feel exhausted or guilty, and they may become conscious that they are emotionally estranged. Both spouses will have to work hard as a team to reconnect. Ask about their interests and their willingness to help. Find out if they're willing to look at ways for coping with detachment-related emotions like anxiety and fear. Here are a few steps on how to stay connected with you partner when encountering challenging times.

Encourage your partner

if you believe that they are suffering from depression or anxiety, to seek support from a mental or a relationship counselor. It is difficult to fight a battle by itself as your partner is also lacking in motivation. Reassure them that seeking help from a professional is a healthy way to cope with tension and emotions. Offer them to be accompanied by a counselor if you have similar sentiments. To ask for help is never too late.

Have a conversation with your partner

Make it clear that you want to hear what they have to say. Show them that you want anything they want to open up. Let them know what you think and feel soft. Talk to them in a friendly way, and encourage them to talk more. Try to have an in-depth discussion on your relationship, your views on changing routines and values which may affect your days ahead. Search for your happiness and any improvements in the relationship they wish to see. Pay attention and process your feelings before reacting. Choose the right words to say and make sure that you understand what they're trying to imply.

·Talk to your partner about the need to be alone. It is essential in a relationship to give each other time and space they needed. Let your partner enjoy his moment alone with music, games or other people intentionally. Encourage the relationship to be entertained in their way of releasing stress. Go check out a new cinema, listen to music and do all your soul's energy when reading a book. Consult them about lending yourself a while, because you should still make time for yourself, because that's how this should be. Relationships are immensely noticeable when both parties are happier and refreshed when seeing them lifting and standing together and for each other. The setting of alone time will help to collect ideas or to clarify your mind. It encourages your thoughts to unite while reflecting. It makes you decide without regrets, and it makes you love your partner without losing yourself.

Examine how you communicate with your partner and the manner in how you deliver it

When you react to your partner, it also affects the way they respond, you can show anger or be excessively critical when talking with them. As a response, they'll also be defensive while replying to you. You do not know that your answer has hurt your partner's feelings. Your opinion, values, and response have a great impact on them. One of my counsel, Justin, is always sensitive to what her partner, Lara, has to say. When Lara is angry, her words sometimes act like a dagger on Justin. That's how it works for a couple. When you truly love someone, you give importance to their views more than yours but if you fail to use the right words, as a consequence, they isolate themselves from you to prevent offending you or being criticized again. When confronting your partner, try to bring positivity, or at least, peacefulness in the conversation. When you can't control your emotions, try being neutral, or directional before you could say something degrading or offensive to them. Being kind with your words acts as an indicator that you won't judge them even if you think that what they did is wrong.

Many couples experience relational problems in their relationships. Emotional disconnection is a red flag that something needs to be discussed and talked through. The only way to solve your problem is by communicating. The importance of discussing the issue is vital to the health of the relationship. When couples decided to leave the problems unaddressed, it serves as a root to more series of problems that could destroy the wellbeing of a relationship. The relationship status becomes suspicious and doubtful and everything feels on hold. It's the problems that keep you from going on with life. Free yourself from the problems and work it out with your partner. The longer you let it be, the more serious destruction it will give. You deserve a romantic relationship that is emotionally satisfying and provides you with the level of intimacy and closeness that you want. It gives you freedom and space to grow. It does not suffocate you to be something that you're not. It is forgiving and lets you grow and bloom beautifully. You're in a healthy relationship when you don't feel less of yourself and you find love everywhere you go.

Takeaway Exercise

Ask the following questions to your partner and exchange answers to determine whether you're making progress in building emotional intimacy with them and which aspects need some improvements.

1. If you could choose the activities to do that would make a perfect day, what would you choose?
2. What amongst your childhood memory is your favorite?

3. When was the last time you cried, and what did you worry about?
4. When do you feel most loved in our relationship?
5. As a child, what was your favorite stuff or hobby to do, and what makes you happy about it?
6. If you could change something about yourself, what would it be?
7. What's something most reminiscing about our dating phase that you wish we could still do right now?
8. Who are the most important persons to you and how much do you value them?
9. Is there something you are grateful for? What is it?

10. How do you imagine having kids in the household? Do you think you'll be a good parent to them?

Chapter 5

Step 4: Build an Interdependent Relationship

Healthy Relationships. What does it mean by practicing a healthy relationship to build an interdependent bond? Most of us grew up knowing the importance of having connections with others, more so when it comes to relationships. We will occasionally come across couples that look so happy together, that close bond, mutual respect, and comfort is something we aspire to have. We should keep in mind that behind a happy relationship is a responsibility that both spouses have to live by. To maintain a healthy relationship, we must face a series of failures because that is where wisdom lies. We humans have a desire for social interaction and that desire is why we value having a connection and a close intimacy with our partner and that's why putting an effort to help that intimacy grow will make your long-term relationships that much easier.

There is a popular misconception of a relationship is that your partner will "fix" you. Although it can be easier to think that once you meet the love of your life, all things that are going wrong will simply resolve, that's just not how things work. Your partner will not be the one to fix you because you are responsible for your being. They may be of help and motivation but you are the one who has to help yourself, even in relationships. To build a healthy relationship and an interdependent one, don't expect that your partner should always be the one who will come up with a solution or put in the effort to fix your problems, they won't always be there. That's why there is something called an interdependent relationship to prevent you or your spouse from fully depending on each other. Going into a relationship and putting those kinds of burdens majorly on your partner is just plain irresponsible and will toxify the relationship later on. Realize that your partner is the one who can provide you an amazing kind of support and guide you along the way, but never expect them to do the work for you.

What is Interdependence?

Interdependence is basically when one or both partners recognizes the importance of having a close intimacy, being actively present in the relationship but without sacrificing their personal goals or sense of self like their personality or morals. They value and respect their own and their partner's sense of self, being able to trust each other and feel close even if they're doing other things, finding the balance between time together and time apart. It is how they learn to be their person whose identity is preserved around his/her relationship, you have your aspirations and values. Your partner should respect that and shouldn't force you to compromise to change. It is where one in which the partners trust each other and work together to preserve harmony in every way possible. In such a partnership, the spouses are independent but not codependent, which means they prioritize the needs and interests of the other. They are working together with the chance of growing individually.

For instance, an interdependent couple knows the importance of showing their weaknesses to support and guide their partner in a way that they don't have to compromise themselves to improve their emotional intimacy. Relationships often fall apart when both parties try to change each other or worse blame their partner for something they lack. An interdependent person respects each other on a deeper level. This sense of respect allows them to continue being themselves without the need to majorly change who they are or what they believe in. It's worth noting that interdependence is different from independence. Both partners need emotional support and as everything goes, being independent when taken too far can become an obstacle to be able to have a deep connection with others rather than an advantage. You will find it difficult to lean on your partner when you're in trouble and that disconnect will lead to fights and misunderstandings. It can be hard for people to learn to lean on others when they went through life being independent but don't worry, it can be unlearned to an extent. When we are with our partners, their opinions, values, and beliefs affect our thinking without us being aware of it. That's why sometimes, people lost their identity when spending most of the time with their partners. They are being defined by them, which is wrong. When you lost yourself amid hardships, it's hard to bring back your individuality even before entering the relationship. That's why building emotional intimacy in relationships will always be difficult to do regularly, as you have to find the balance between being independent and showing vulnerabilities, leaning on your partner for support and guidance.

Why is interdependence healthy in a relationship?

Contrary to the popular belief, spending time apart from your partner is also important to the relationship. It's practically normal and healthy to have separate times for hobbies and other social relationships like family and friends. Being able to give each other time and space is a sign of mutual respect and trust. After having time apart, your soul will feel refreshed and maybe even excited to share your experiences apart with them. Spending time apart is beneficial in the relationship as a whole. The essence of longing reflects the importance of a relationship that stimulates our solitude to recharge from everything which could lead to cherishing our partners more. Doing things alone that can make you happy is not being selfish, it's a sign that you care about the relationship. You wanted the relationship to stay fresh and alive like the first time, and there's no struggling in feeling obligated to be with them all day.

Healthy interdependence is when the relationship is great for both partners with both their needs are being fulfilled and support each other in better ways. You have full control over your personal space which can avoid further arguments. Having space and time for hobbies and other things is important but at the same time, you also feel that you're happiest and more relaxed when enjoying quality time together. The good thing about interdependence is that you can still be the person you always were. You can't be happy just by being around one person all the time. Life is a continuous journey and it required new experiences in life. But when your happiness depends on them, it pressures them a lot too. After all, what could be better than hanging out with your biggest fan, closest friend, lover, and partner in crime after long days of not communicating with them?

How to build an Interdependent Relationship?

Most of us value our romantic relationship as the most valuable one. We tend to create bonds of love and intimacy with someone dear to our heart. However, long-term relationships are far from that. It does not only depend on a couple's emotional connection but it creates a safe, secure, and it guarantees us our freedom to explore more. An interdependent person gives significance to their sensitivity and vulnerability. They don't hide behind their partner's identity and maintains a sense of knowing themselves. Being reliant on another person can seem frightening or even unhealthy. We are shaped with exaggerated importance of freedom, to be somewhat self-sufficient, and to put a high value on not imposing emotional support from others.

Think about it, when someone has that strong aura of self-independence, they often look powerful, influential, and charismatic. They are often the center of attraction because they look overwhelming in a direct way. They can communicate with empathy and yet they are known as rational and logical. Maybe that's why most people hate powerful men or women. Because they have known their weakness and they make use of it by building a strong character in which one can be shaken. Interdependence can be difficult to achieve especially if you're someone who does not value independence or maintains a hateful sense of superiority over your partner. Within the partnership, interdependence encompasses a balancing of self and others, with all partners striving to be present and meet each other's physical and emotional needs in acceptable and meaningful ways. Partners do not ask each other and don't seek their partner's feelings of dignity. This encourages each partner to maintain their feelings of self and also to advance and interfere in times of dire need of help. It also enables them, beyond fear of repercussions, to make certain choices.

To establish an interdependent relationship is essential to know who you are from the outset. People also only get into such relationships to escape the sentiment of being single without appreciating self-love, values, ideals, and other qualities that make you special to someone else. That's how your own identity is all about. It requires your desire to work and to develop your relationship. Take the time to track who you were once. To develop the development of an interdependent relationship it is important to possess such knowledge. It is important, according to certified psychotherapist Sharon Martin, LCSW, to retain a sense of self in your interpersonal relationship. The following techniques to maintain the sense of oneself in a relationship are recommended:

·Being mindful of your values and beliefs in life.

When you have taken the time to understand and learn more about what you believe in, it will naturally affect how important those values are to you. You may feel intimidated by others or simply want to avoid any sort of confrontation, but you should learn when to act and stand your ground. Learning that what you believe in is a major part of who you are as it plays an essential part in your mindset. It will be a sign that you respect yourself and a form of self-love. Each person's morals and beliefs are the roots of their identity and being respectful to both your partner's and your own beliefs instead of forcing anyone to conform to their beliefs can give a clearer path for an interdependent relationship.

·Voicing out your thoughts and feelings.

Keeping your opinions, impressions, and judgments grounded can help build your confidence as you speak louder than your head. One of the most peaceful feelings is the feeling of being heard, being able to express yourself fully, like truth, can set you free. When you are offended by something your partner has done, address them and speak yourself up. That's also how you can introduce yourself to other people, and leave a strong sense of identity and impression to them. Sometimes, people are easily deterred by someone who is emotionally strong and intelligent. You cannot beat someone who knows their worth. They know when to stand up for themselves, and you must respect that as their partner. Don't even hesitate if you want clarifications. It avoids possible arguments and leads to a more open and honest relationship.

·Conserving the confidence to ask for what you deserve.

When you know your worth, you are not easily trembled by your negative thoughts. You know when to walk away, when to back off, and when to stop allowing other people to take advantage of you. Unite with the power of your voice to ask for what you deserve. Settling for less won't bring you the peace of satisfaction. On the other hand, authorize your partner to feel confident about themselves. Unravel your desires in life, and work together to secure that purpose, whether it may be an object or feeling, it will always be valid because that's how your mind reacts to certain things, but if you react to something conflictingly, recognize your fault and find ways to work on yourself to be able to give your partner the same confidence as well.

·Enjoying leisure time with family and friends.

One of the things that will help you be a better partner is spending time with family and friends and letting yourselves miss each other. By letting each other keep up with their other social relationships and doing the things they love like interests or hobbies is a form of self-care. It will naturally make the both of you happier and it will lighten the relationship just the same. It will make your relationship only stronger because both partners will feel more fulfilled, giving new experiences and memories to share and be happy about.

·Continuing your dreams and goals

As we've established, you are your person even before the relationship started. You have your dreams and ambitions. Never let the relationship define you and most of all, sacrifice those dreams and ambitions for it. A relationship is a place where you feel safe, happy, and motivated to improve. It should be a boost to help you reach your dreams, not chains that will keep you down and disillusioned. You shouldn't sacrifice your goals just for the sake of keeping your partner happy. It will only shift the balance of control, making the relationship unhealthy and co- dependent. Interdependent relationships shouldn't force changes but guide and encourage improvements, helping their partners to move forward to their goals not keep them on a stagnant cliff with nowhere to go but with you.

·Getting comfortable of declining or saying "no" when needed.

Anytime you agree to something when you don't want to will lead to resentment, which can negatively affect your relationship. Knowing when to speak your opinions and saying no is a sign of respect to the relationship. Because you're showing honesty and being true to your partner, qualities that all healthy relationships encourage and want. It also encourages your partner to do the same, setting an example of how important this is.

The more you practice, the more comfortable you'll be to say no and set up boundaries. As you grow more confident, the more likely you'll be able to stand your ground in more intense situations. For example, when your partner wants something from you that you can't give or want to do. To encourage the relationship to be more honest, true, and free from bitterness. Providing your spouse' space and freedom to retrieve their sense of self is essential to building a safe and interdependent relationship. Rebuild a relationship that allows you to create a safe personal space where partners can celebrate the re-freshness of the relationship without feeling compelled to do so. It reduces the worry about losing oneself and avoids emotional coercion. It protects its partners' preciousness which attracts a tranquil atmosphere in which they are not guilty and anger each other. Take the time and think about who you are and what is best for you in your relationship. Let this remind you that dating is a process and should guarantee that it has a firm, stable basis such that your romance is strengthened in the long run.

Maintain a sense of self-identity

You need to comprehend that your relationship doesn't define you. Before you even started dating, you were hanging out with your friends, made some time for your hobbies, and did fun activities. You have your own life and that should not end once you enter a relationship, you only share the experience with your partner and that can make you happier. Your partner is not allowed to limit, or even restrict the things you once did before being with them. But that doesn't give you the right from avoiding to improve and change. If that hobby could destroy something in a relationship, maybe it's better to accept the help they're offering to overcome it. A close friend of mine had a relationship where they would always do things together. They dropped their friends and even interests to have more time together, and it went great for a while. However, after time has passed, they were constantly at each other's throats, which is unhealthy and sickening. I advised them to spend some time away from each other and go back to someone you've identified as your character before being with them. It doesn't matter whether he's dating, in a long-term relationship, or even married. By spending time apart, they both wouldn't have to sacrifice their sense of self and always have something to share after. He talked it through with his girlfriend who was surprised at first but understood that it was becoming a problem too, they are in a much better situation now, spending 3 years of their lives together and apart. Remember that you had a life before getting in a relationship. When introducing yourself, you don't say, "Nice to meet you, I'm John's girlfriend" You already built a character of your own and you should strengthen it to maintain a better personality.

Keep track of your personal goals.

You had your life before entering a relationship

with them. You desire a dream, in which you are loved and successful. Do not forget to keep track of your personal goals and live by the dream you wanted for yourself. Being in a relationship does not give you the limitation of being you. Keep your fighting spirit alive by reasoning out and looking back on times when you struggled to get there. You are still your person. You have the freedom of yesterday, today, and tomorrow. It doesn't inevitably mean that you should break up with your partner because it's you who thought you could only do too little by being with them. Let your partner be part of your goal. Seek moral support and guidance. They might know about something related to your dream job or career. Use them to drive your motivation back because they should be a part of your story.

Be respectful of each other's morals and values.

Remember what made you attracted to your partner in the first place. Take a good look at the bigger picture and not nitpick on the differences. Try to focus on their positive qualities rather and you'll give yourself the room to appreciate and love all the things that make your partner awesome and recognize why you're so in love with them. If both of you try to stop trying to change each other and make them live up to your "ideal" partner, you will automatically remove most sources of arguments. You shouldn't try to change them but you encourage them to grow and improve. Keep the soles of their feet steering in the direction towards their whole being, their identity. Accept the morals and values that they lived by, and aspire to acceptance from them. As the saying goes, "respect begets respect". It should come in both ways. Acceptance is the key to respect. Accepting that they are the way they are before you even came into their lives is vital. Avoid thinking that they wouldn't be right where they are right now because of you. You don't even want someone displaying superiority so stop acting like one. Instead, share each other's values, morals, and beliefs and try to work on it when you disagree about that matter.

Be comfortable being apart and together.

The key to a balanced healthy relationship is to make yourself comfortable attaining a sense of individuality freely. Imagine when you went on a trip overseas to de-stress yourself and cleanse your soul. While being on that trip, you realized that you and your partner have been getting on each other's nerves for a long time. It's like a breath of fresh air or eating a craving that you've been longing for a long time. That's not because your partner is toxic and problematic, it's because there's

no space between the relationship and your privacy is continuously being invaded while not realizing you're invading theirs too. These are the common reasons why most relationships don't last. They ended up suffocating each other. They forgot that they need to breathe and let out the toxic routine they voluntarily let themselves into. On the other hand, imagine going on a refreshing trip, and before heading back home, you realized you miss your partner and you can't wait to embrace them any longer. Keep the spirit of eagerness alive and train yourself to relieve the tension while being apart and even more relaxed by being together.

Interdependence Vs. Co-dependency.

What is Co-dependency?

Interdependence and Co-dependence may seem similar but they are very different. Co- dependence is when emotional support is taken to an extreme and becomes an almost daily necessity. A co-dependent partner is someone who heavily relies on their partners and held them accountable for their self and well-being. They also make any sacrifice whether it's cutting off friends or family, dropping any hobbies, and even goals or dreams. In worst cases, it almost comes off as obsessiveness. Mutual support is the cornerstone of an interdependent partnership. These features help the partners' development as a team. The codependent relationship, on the other hand, is all about power and influence. It's like feeling superior and displaying constant dominance over your partner. As a consequence, the relationship is unbalanced and unhealthy. A couple that is interdependent shares obligations and is aware of each other's needs. However, in a codependent relationship, one partner is normally the controller, while the other is the managed or follower. The imbalance is visible. The spouse is not allowed to complain or grasp his/her freedom as their partner is manipulative. Codependent relationships are unhealthy because they do not encourage partners to be self-sufficient or to develop. One or both partners depend heavily on each other and the relationship in these dysfunctional relationships for their self-conception, dignity, and overall emotional wellbeing. If a connection does not work out, one or both partners may feel sickening and start worrying about things that don't even need to be worried about.

What is the difference between Interdependency and Co-dependency?

Interdependence boosts partner trust and self-esteem while also encouraging feelings of emotional protection and mutual respect. Codependency is more about putting one's attention on themselves rather than on one's partner. Individuals in an interdependent relationship are free to be themselves, whereas those in a codependent relationship are forced to change or even compromise for the sake of the other. As a result, unlike a codependent relationship, the interdependent relationship is balanced and stable. Staying in a codependent relationship keeps the partner from being themselves and they unwillingly portray a version of a person that will never be them. A meaningful and healthy relationship encourages the growth and development of an individual. A couple must be interdependent to have a lasting partnership and experience development with each other. Codependency can be negative, and it's likely won't last in the long run. By keeping to the features of an interdependent connection, you will open the windows of satisfaction and see how happy your life is.

Why is Co-dependency unhealthy for a relationship?

It's unhealthy because it promotes one or both partners to only feel like a whole person with their partner and always compromise for the other without thinking for their own needs or interests. It may start great at first but as time goes on, those habits of depending on the other for support will show the problems that had been slowly building up. It's simply unhealthy because you constantly sacrifice your sense of self and the authenticity of who you are, as the foundation of the relationship becomes fear rather than happiness. It's also unhealthy for the reason that it can be a way to directly manipulate your partner without even noticing that you are, as they depend on you for help and do more for you and less for themselves. It becomes a relationship where it focuses on pleasing our partner for self-worth and meaning while also blocking self-growth and slowly sacrifice ourselves making the relationship lose meaning in the first place. Because, they fell in love and come to know you as you and if you start to sacrifice your own life, interests, and goals. It will only push the both of you further apart. If a partnership becomes codependent, it easily devolves into unstable territory, with a lack of control and authenticity. According to licensed psychotherapist Renae Helms, the issues begin to emerge when we cross the line from loving to codependent, and the relationship becomes fear-based. When we lose our sense of self, we can no longer be ourselves and must rely on the outside world to give us a sense of self and value. We are being displayed behind someone's shadow. Therefore, there's no growth and a sense of familiarity with who we are. According to research on codependency, "a codependent's very damaging behavior of placing others' needs ahead of their own needs can undermine both participants' healthy mental and emotional development." Depression, withdrawal, anxiety, and even the persistence of the dependent codependent cycle are all signs of codependency" (Waughfield, 2002). This clearly explains that codependent persons are putting the blame on their partners and refused to take any encouragement to change because they are fine with that behavior. Avoid being taken advantage of, and be respectful of your individuality. Do not settle in a relationship that is toxic enough to prevent you from knowing the truth. Attract people with the same goal as you in a relationship, and strive for making things better, peaceful and loving in your life. Be with someone who values a unique piece of art like you, and someone who sees your starry night as beautiful as your golden daylight.

Takeaway Exercise

This is an interactive exercise that requires partners to exchange answers to the following question and assess each other's interdependency.

1. Do you feel the need to be alone?
2. Do you feel the need to control others? Do you consider yourself a leader or a follower?
3. Where do you get your ideas inspired from?
4. Do you think you are inadequate, equal, or better than other people?
5. Do you rely on others for help?

Reference:https://www.quotev.com/quiz/660585/Are-you-codependent-independent-or- interdependent

Chapter 6

Step 5: Rekindle your Relationship

It's common for people to fall out of love and wanting to end their relationship sooner. For some, it was full of toxicity, sadness, and anxiety. For some, it taught them lessons they never knew they needed. It was a happy yet tragic love story. It was beautiful, filled with happy moments, butterflies, and familiar comfort. There is nothing more amazing than being mesmerized the first time you laid your eyes off your partner, enjoying their presence a lot, and feeling their heartbeats in the silence. For a reason, there is a common ground to why people fall out of love without knowing how to figure that out for themselves, making their partner feel more fear and anxiety. Have you ever begun starting a fire? Staring at its astounding flame as the sparks of ashes starts wandering around? Any burning fire started in a small domain until it starts creating a massive barrage. When it's continuously being fed with chunks of woods and sticks, it continues releasing light and heat for an amount of time, but when someone disregarded it, it rapidly disappears until it dies out. That's the same concept that we're trying to apply in our relationships. Think of your relationships like lighting a fire. With the right materials, you can easily make that small spark into a strong burst of flame and what comes after is entirely up to you. However, giving a relationship too much of your time and effort, much like giving fire too much kindle, and can be destructive to not only the ones involved but to others around it, much like your other social relationships. While exerting little effort on your relationship, is much like neglecting the fire and it will slowly weaken and die out. Both situations tell how much have you improved even up to reading this page, it will reflect what you do want in the relationship, and what aspects need more attention and improvement. We should try to balance everything out, giving it the right amount of time and effort, much like giving a flame the proper amount of kindle and protection, and in turn, it will be a comforting warmth and a protective light. This light will serve as the guide to the happy ending of your path you're currently exploring.

How to rekindle an extinguished relationship?

As any relationship grows and matures, the effort given to sustain that emotional intimacy slowly fades away, making the spark that kept you going die out. This is a common sign that the relationship needs improvement. The relationship's standard requires a higher level of intimacy, which in return, should be provided with our partners. It's natural to anticipate something more in a relationship, it means that you are looking forward to giving more effort to them through the intimacy that you can furnish. Most relationships fall into a false sense of comfort and go into an almost daily routine. At first, it can give both a feeling of safety and security in the relationship, but without anything new in the relationship, the spark may die down due to a lack of excitement and new experiences. Our heads will constantly disturb us to learn and explore something new because it needs nourishing. On the other hand, even if your relationship is in this phase, it can still go better. As long as both of you are willing to put in the time and effort, they hope to make the spark grow does not fade. You may need to have the motivation to get through the issues you're currently avoiding. If you start to drift away from your partner, it's nothing that regular communication, showing of vulnerabilities, love, and reconnection can't fix. But, before we get into detailed instructions on how to rekindle your relationship, we first need to understand why they die out in the first place. We need to recall how did such a lovely atmosphere fade out of our awareness. The only reason that we can move forward is to know our past, and what has caused such a destructive occurrence. One of the most common reasons why the spark was extinguished is because of our lack of interdependence and communication, which is an essential key to any relationship's success. It's either you are drifting away or you are insisting yourself on them too much which prohibits space to meddle in between. When there's a lack of communication and intimacy, all the other problems constantly arise.

The most popular reason that you have to recharge the flame is that you both have stopped making the effort to maintain your friendship alive. You're lonely in the relationship, so you stop trying to leave things as it is. You may have avoided talking to each other respectfully or started to threaten each other for mistakes. Maybe because you have spent so much time at work or with your buddies you pulled away from your other. It is hard to manage life transitions for many couples. They finished the link. They fail to respond to the improvements that are necessary to remain linked. But don't worry, even though you offer more explanations or excuses why you want to revitalize your friendship, it doesn't matter. It is all that matters that it is necessary. If you'd like to work on changing a broken relationship, whether it is a modern kind of dating or a long love affair, you will need some emotional enlightenment. The subsequent incremental changes will lead to significant results over time and continue to rekindle the flames.

Find the right harmony and balance of the relationship.

Have you ever heard of yin and yang? It's a concept in ancient Chinese philosophy that for life to be balanced, there should be an opposite to everything as per the established notion of dualism. Where there is attraction, there should be disconnection, where there is intimacy, there should be solitude. You certainly have considerable experience having similar stuff with your spouse, you still come to one conclusion and remain united to decision-making circumstances. We must agree, however, that opposites are equally beautiful. This is all about polarity. There's good and bad, love and hate, right and wrong, weaknesses and strengths. The outcome of something lies in you and your partner's attitude on how you view it. When I was a child, I used to wonder why evil and darkness exist in this world. Can't just God stop them from existing? That's what it called harmony. To have a harmonious life, we must remind ourselves that these things were created to coexist. Can you live in the coldness of the winter without desiring the warmth of summer? It would make us die. We can't live on doing the same routine forever. We must learn how to embrace dualism because it's what helps us to fully appreciate the good in the world and live in the moment. When we're experiencing rainy days, it makes us happy when the sun shines. Consider the first time that you met your partner. The relationship was simple and your immediate interests were seen by physical affection. Reminiscence of this sparkle, ease, and pleasure in reviving a friendship. It will encourage the brain to remember when and how you fall in love with them. Keep the natural environment, loving energy, and self-love confidence. You bloomed like a flower and smiles like a ray of sunshine. Your partner is always drawn to you even in your normal dress-up and natural state. Your relationship is made up of chemistry by the combination of your natural resources with your partner's power. When you work with each other in a natural, balanced manner, you do not mask your true selves and should be fulfilled where you are. If you are in a position to restore a relationship, you will almost inevitably realize either or both of you having misplaced your true selves in the middle, and recovering this vitality is vital to success.

Maintain physical intimacy with your partner.

When hard times approach our relationship, we tend to avoid our partner in any circumstances possible. We have problems resisting our ego and our other major ones are emotional. This is a typical issue in a partnership where sex is a dispute. Either you penalize your partner for less romantic treatment or for whatever reason refuse intercourse, you have to remedy it immediately. When you or both cannot show physical love, you cannot recover a relationship practically. It is through physical intimacy that we feel loved and enough. When our partner adores our body, it brings positive effects to our soul mentally and emotionally as well. We feel assured that they also feel the desire of the moment. It boosts our dopamine or happy hormones as well as the excitement which can help us to get into the best possible shape to reignite our passion. Affectionate intimacy, whether sexual or not, give our significant other a warm comforting caress, that a single touch can simply mean, "I'm here. I won't leave you" gestures that leave a strong impact on your partner. I do not even say sex doesn't matter. Naturally, sex plays an important role in a relationship and it is important to recognize your sexual energy and the energy of your partner to build a new relationship. Effective sex education leads to good sex, better comprehension, and a closer relationship with your partner. Since you know your body can articulate what you desire, your happiness is increased. And knowing your partner's body gives you more faith in your ability to satisfy them, which strengthens your relationship. You also stop feeling broken because you know what turns you on when you know who you are erotic. You keep yourself secure emotionally and physically when you have clear boundaries and can discuss them with your partner. If you're finding that your sexual intimacy is dwindling, you need to act now before it becomes an insurmountable issue. When you don't have guilt, you are wiser to be who you are: someone who is physically delighted cultivates romantic passion and gets deeper joy and satisfaction out of life. And when you are enjoying sex at this stage, you have richer, more rewarding relationships and interactions, which equates to more progress in this life.

Display curiosity in your partner's life.

When we started dating our partners, we are immensely curious about their personal life and experiences. We wanted to know how did it shape who they are now. We wanted to know what's going on inside their heads and what are their thoughts during 2 AM. We have this weird impression of knowing what they are thinking and feeling at all times. We asked questions about their childhood and future goals. Do you still behave the same way? Are you as curious about his life as before? If not, it may be one of the reasons you're now trying to figure out how to rekindle love. Your curiosity decreases as you know information about them which shouldn't be stopped. Seasons changes like people. If you're not displaying curiosity about the happenings in their life, they will feel that you are becoming more uninterested in them. The efforts are inconsistent which makes the relationship boring. Curiosity about your partner entails asking questions and listening carefully as they respond. It goes beyond inquiring about their day or what they want to eat for dinner. Find out what they think about current affairs, how their new job makes them feel about their life goals, and how their plans have changed. Fixing a relationship becomes simpler for both of you when you pique your interest in your partner. In the previous chapters, we've talked about listening attentively to your partner, understanding where they are coming from, and showing your empathy towards their feeling.

Be an active presence and listen

Now, I'd like to emphasize what it means to practice deep listening when communicating with them. Have you ever talked to someone who made you feel like you were the only person in the universe at that moment? Who seemed genuinely involved and interested in every word that came out of your mouth? What was your reaction to that? How did that make you feel? Deep listening has this kind of strength. Deep listening is a transformative communication technique as well as a beneficial social habit. Deep listening not only gives you the time and space to completely absorb what your conversation partner is saying, but it also encourages your conversation partner to feel understood and talk more freely and honestly. And this is a vital step in building a relationship with others. When someone is listening attentively to us, it makes us want to converse more or even have a close friendship with them. We wanted to be heard like that forever! I remember when my mentor teaches us how to develop deep listening, when our curiosity is driven by something, we don't realize how we want them to tell us something more. We learn and comprehend every word that comes out of their mouth like magic. Their eye contact tells us that they are fully engaged and interested in what we're saying. One of the Leadership Academy language expert, Jan Hargave, listed out 4 core principles of deep listening as:

1. **Making eye contact with your partner.**
You show your conversation partner that you are completely involved and interested in what he or she is saying by ensuring good eye contact. The 80/20 rule, which states that you should meet your speaking partner's eyes 80% of the time and wander 20% of the time while you gather information to suggest, is a reasonable rule to obey.
2. **Establishing a comfortable presence.**
The average individual speaks between 135 and 160 words per minute, but their brains function at a rate of 400 to 600 words per minute. This means that your mind is running ahead of your conversation partner's mouth, making it possible for your mind to wander. It's up to you to keep your mind from wandering and to be com-

pletely involved in the discussion. You will not only be able to fully comprehend what your partner says, but you will also be able to answer in kind, making them feel valued and acknowledged.

3. **Avoiding nonverbal feedback.**
Nothing is more frustrating than conversing with someone who does not respond verbally. It's as though you're speaking to a brick wall. Attempt to acknowledge your conversation partner with a nod, smile, or other indication of acknowledgment. These nonverbal signals can seem insignificant, but they have a significant impact by demonstrating your interest, comprehension, and participation in the conversation.

4. **Forming a connection.**

When interacting with someone one-on-one, place the body in such a way that it provides a comfortable and supportive environment for him or her to express themselves freely. Lean in slightly, open your chest, draw your shoulders back, and softly fold your hands in your lap or on the table in front of you. Shape a reversed hand steeple with your fingers coming together to form a point if you're standing. When someone steeples in the lap field, it indicates that they are secure in their hearing.

Evolve and place the best commitment into the relationship

You and your spouse used to show each other your best sides when you were first dating. Showing them your strengths and connections in life or something that makes you apart from all their past lovers. You spend most of your time always thinking about ways to make your partner feel exceptional, such as thinking for a sentimental gift, writing love letters, or arranging romantic dates. You were, above all, your partner's biggest fan, and they were yours. You adore everything they do, and you seem to be in a good mood when you're in their company. When did this end, and how did it respond to your desire to learn how to rekindle a relationship? You can place yourself in the optimistic, caring, and relationship-focused mindset that is required to create a solid, dedicated, and stable partnership by concentrating on building a raving fan culture at home. Supporting each other's plans, dreams, and goals is one way to nurture each other. Be your lover's no. 1 fan and show your support more than ever. The motivation it gives is more than what you would expect. Sometimes, they may be on the verge of giving up, until they found out that one person still believes in them, that person is you. One of the most sentimental gifts you and to your spouse and yourself is to support their passion. Since your partner will return the favor, the partnership will enter a positive loop, strengthening and growing your bond. It's easy to become complacent in a partnership and just fulfill the bare minimum of expectations for becoming a "successful partner." Creating a supportive culture at home, on the other hand, necessitates constantly going above and beyond what your partner expects. When you go above and above to surprise and delight your spouse, they will return the favor with loyalty and adoration. They wouldn't know that they can do so much than what they believe they can because of simple assistance. You have to consider dating someone you're in a serious relationship with. You can keep the spark and enthusiasm alive by planning dates with your partner or even surprising him or her. Likewise, expressing your gratitude for having your partner in your life will help. Make it clear to your wife that you enjoy her business. Or tell your husband how fortunate you are to have him in your life. Tell him of the value he adds to your life. Compliment him, pay attention to him, and let your husband know that he is important to you. Your companion is entitled to your undivided attention, which involves getting personal interaction. Evolving in a relationship is a must because change is necessary, and it often results in disputes and claims. This is particularly true when people feel unheard, disrespected, or ignored. Different periods of life necessitate multiple emotional criteria. This is why you should focus on improving yourself and discover new and powerful ways to fulfill your partners' needs and wants in a relationship. We need to understand that we need to innovate and put forward extraordinary effort for the bond to continue to strengthen and deepen. When you start putting time into a more mature relationship from the beginning, fixing a relationship almost takes care of itself.

Use the right words to console your partner

Your words are almost as important as physical intimacy and thoughtfulness in a relationship. Your words have such influence, for those looking for ways to rekindle a relationship may not know that the words they've been using for their partner are hurting them. It can help your partner feel worse or better. It's like a poison in which a single sentence can have such an impact on someone. Not only can the stories we tell ourselves describe us as people, but our words can also either strengthen or weaken our partner and partnership. There is no right thing to say in certain situations because we are living in our perspective. Everything that comes based on our thinking and perspective is called an opinion. What makes the difference is the honesty of you and your partner. One of these cases is learning how to rekindle love, and to do that, you must learn to interact successfully with your partner. Perfection is the lowest possible standard someone can set on something as it leaves no room for improvement. Although perfecting a job may feel good for a short time, it is through our failures that we grow our greatest strengths and learn life's most important lessons. You haven't learned much until you've accomplished anything well until you've learned how to perform this job differently, for example, or what to stop. You're limiting your capabilities by convincing yourself you have to be fine. You must give up perfection if you want to learn how to turn your life around. To do that, we must accept that our relationship will never be perfect but it can be happy. Rather than aiming for a perfect relationship, aim for a well- balanced life. Accept that you can make mistakes, and when you do, use them to propel yourself to the next level. Fear of loss motivates people to strive for perfection. Rather than being scared of failing, follow your passion regardless of the outcome. When talking with your partner, whether it's about your ride to the grocery store or settling a personal dispute, use heartfelt and genuine words. Don't forget to say "I love you," "thank you," and "I miss you," and other encouraging words among other stuff. These little words, when spoken with sincere feelings, make difficult times between you two simpler, allowing you to create or restore faith after it has been betrayed. When I and my husband first became a couple, I always wonder why he utters "I love you" too often. As a hopeless romantic, I value the word "I love you" because it means that you'll take any risk just to be with me and you've decided to keep my soul company forever. I tried confronting him why, and he says that it's his make to make me feel that

I am deserving of love. It makes me realize how this brings a positive impact on my emotional and mental state when he comforts me like that. I never knew I needed that kind of affirmation and that's what love is all about. Speaking with so much care and sensitivity even amid arguments can avoid blame at all costs. When you're debating, don't mention something you'll regret later when you're in the heat of the moment. Remind yourself that this is a person you care for and trust and that your comments have a significant impact on them. You will discover that your rekindled love is much deeper than the love you shared at the start of your relationship when you work together to express your love and admiration for each other.

Create a treasure trove of fond memories

Each pair is facing harsh times and bad interactions are easy to dwell on. Especially when we are driven by our emotions and we tend to forget all the memories we have shared with our partner. The most flexible way is to create a healthy memory bank to counter these challenges you can think of when you fail. When you concentrate on pleasure and attachment moments, these emotions are restored and passion is rekindled. Where you focus your attention is where your energy flows. Plan routine dates and identifies special times to construct your memory bank.

Search for some excuse to rejoice, even if it is planned suddenly or for no reason. Build rituals that comfort and strengthen your relationship. The memory bank you're about to create can help you find the relationship's purpose. It will remind you of the challenges you once shared with your partner and how did you overcome it. Treat each other with compassion and sensitivity and take any opportunity you can to build your partner up. It is not easy to learn how to revitalize a relationship but it will worth everything in the end. It takes time and work to build and maintain a strong and stable relationship and much longer if you face a fractured relationship. However, you can restore trust and bond emotionally with your partner with time and maturity. It is not simple to master how to help revive a relationship. It takes time and effort to develop and sustain a solid and steady relationship. That being said, you can regain trust and connect with time and experience emotionally with your partner.

Takeaway Exercise

The first column lists many aspects of life. Brainstorm objectives you want to accomplish with any dimension. There are no limitations on the amount or purpose of the objectives you mention. You are brainstorming. Identify objectives in the second column and targets in the third column you would like to target. Since your time and resources are limited, the number of targets you set is normally helpful. Take into account your objectives in your first step. Have that in the objectives in another column, remember that your answers will eventually be compared to your spouse's objectives and acceptance. Compare the Step 1 table with the table of your partner. Discuss your targets first. Give each other suggestions about their worthiness and ways on how you can achieve it.

Dimension	Personal Goal Ideas	Couple Goal Ideas
Financial		
Household		
Physical		
Social		
Spiritual		
Marriage and Personal Enrichment		

Conclusion

Conclusion

Relationships are easy to manage, but you have to try to learn how to cope with every challenge life would throw at you and your partner. This book serves as a reminder that dwelling on the negative side of the relationship won't equate to leaving the person who witnessed your hardship and worst days but still chose to stay. Remember all the workouts we learned whenever you're on the verge of a stiff cliff again. All these are simple activities that any pair can do daily, but it is much harder to act on and make it a common practice because each pair is distinct and each pair needs to concentrate on a certain number of factors. Some couples need to focus on communication, some need to focus on their individuality and time or space apart. Some couples have all the bases covered but lack that emotional intimacy to grow it further and couples who don't have anything wrong with them at all but simply aren't compatible. There's also the fact that every problem cannot be solved, learn to accept rather than damage your relationship on forcing that can't be solved. Don't focus on your differences or what the both of you lack, you can certainly try but it's better to focus on what makes your partner great and improve on it. It requires both partners to take the time and understand each other to make a relationship strive and grow, and just the fact you bought this book is proof of your effort and motivation to make your relationship stay strong. You just have to make your partner see your point of view as you should to them. To move forward, we must learn to appreciate the darkness of the past. We need to understand where the problem came from and how did it affect our mental and emotional well-being in an instant. When we choose to leave these conflicts unresolved, it's I'm the relationship that suffers. Affection fades, love diminishes, intimacy was declining. The relationship was tested during these times but always find one reason amid hundreds of negative thoughts overwhelming your entire system. There is a reason that everything of this is happening. It is meant to shape and help us grow. Seeking help doesn't make you less for your partner. We need someone to support and motivate us throughout the way and that is our partner. However, if you and your spouse were deeply affected by the havoc one must step up and sustain encouragement for both. Our baskets will never be empty, choosing how to make the most out of every day makes the difference. Even just reminding your partner how much you adore them leaves a positive impact on their day. Know the relationship's weakness and work on it. Reminisce the times of stress-free and satisfying days you once shared, recall the feeling, and let it serves as our motivation to keep going. It makes the relationship stronger when faith is bigger than suspicions. The most essential key to reviving the relationship is to restart and know your partner again like before, communicate with them, and be educated on how their mind works which are sometimes factored by their childhood and past experiences. Learn the art of grasping everything before giving feedback, and listening attentively to what message is your partner trying to convey. Even in the hardest times or arguments, communicate with them. Avoid attacking your partner and uttering about "keepings scores" and start focusing on the main problem itself. Giving them enough space and time to comprehend and reflect everything results in a healthy argument. Understand how to establish an interdependent relationship to avoid keeping score, and promote open and honest communication. Throughout writing this book, I also experienced the same negative feeling of losing my motivation to write. Would be it worth it to publish this? Will I be able to help a lot of struggling couples like how once we were? That's the thought I had at the back of my head. But then I refuse to be played by my senseless thoughts and emotions. Sometimes, you wouldn't realize there's something deeper than feeling down. It holds your soul on the ground, leaving you unproductive with your life. When that time comes, take a deep breath and give it some time. Retrace the reasons on what had motivated you to fix something or even with the relationship with your partner, even if it takes forever. Trust me, all of the frustrations you've cried out when you feel like giving up will all be worth it. The people that you need are around you. You are surrounded by love because you are supposed to be loved. Seek help from your partner, give the same assistance to them. Work together to find solutions and ways to nurture the relationship. Everything done through God's ways and plans cannot fail. Make him the center of your relationship and he shall help you clean your minds and heart by giving spiritual guidance to make an effective, rational decision through his grace. When you entered this journey, you are never alone. Your partner is with you even in the worst possible chaos of the relationship, and that's what love is. It does not center on the happy times of the relationship, rather, it emphasizes the problems that can make the bond stronger. It provides us with pearls of wisdom that can change how we view life and our relationship. Refuse to be caught by the thoughts that do not even matter. Instead, think of plans in which you can make them happy today. Make them a good breakfast, an avocado toast, kiss them, and a simple "I love you" reminder. There are endless options on how can you make your partner feel precious and nurtured and one of them is choosing to be with them at the end of the day. The strongest relationships are shaped by the most challenging obstacle. Welcome these problems with an open- arms and get ready to take on another journey with your partner. Don't forget to fasten your seatbelts!

References

Paul, Ph. D, M. (n.d.). *What Makes Love Fade In Long-Term Relationships? A Psychologist Explains*. Mind Body Green. Retrieved March 15, 2003, from https://www.mindbodygreen.com/articles/what-makes-love-fade-in-long-term-relationships

Emery, L. R. (2018, August 14). *Why Does Love Fade Over Time? We Asked Experts & Here's What They Said*. Bustle. https://www.bustle.com/p/why-does-love-fade-over-time-we- asked-experts-heres-what-they-said-10024806

Peterson, J. D., & Krane, G. (2012, January 23). *Motivating Your Partner to Improve the Relationship*. Couple Wise. https://couplewise.com/motivating-your-partner-to-improve- the-relationship/

Lindis, C. (n.d.) *Signs You're Losing the Spark in Your Relationship*. Retrieved March 16, 2021, from https://www.lindiscourtney.com/blog/signs-you-are-losing-the-spark-in-your-relationship

Hanekom, G. (n.d.). *How to Stay Motivated to Keep Going When Facing Relationship Challenges*. The Relationship Guy. Retrieved March 18, 2021, from https://therelationshipguy.com/how-to-stay-motivated-to-keep-going-when-facing-relationship-challenges/

Howard, L. (2017, November 15). *9 Signs You're Not Putting Enough Effort Into Your Relationship, According To Experts*. Bustle. https://www.bustle.com/p/9-signs-youre-not- putting-enough-effort-into-your-relationship-according-to-experts-3905256

Herrin, T. (2021, March 10). *How To Recognize Emotional Disconnect In Your Relationship And What To Do To Reconnect*. Regain. https://www.regain.us/advice/general/how-to-recognize-emotional-disconnect-in-your-relationship-and-what-to-do-to-reconnect/

Paavilainen, H. (n.d.). *How to Feel Close and Connected in Your Relationship Again*. Tiny Buddha. Retrieved March 30, 2021, from https://tinybuddha.com/blog/how-to-feel-close- connected-in-relationships/

Clarke, MA, LPC/MHSP, J., & Snyder, MD, C. (2020, October 3). *How to Build a Relationship Based on Interdependence*. Very Well Mind. https://www.verywellmind.com/how-to-build-a-relationship-based-on-interdependence-4161249

Thakur, S., & Carmona-Goyena (Ph.D, Psychotherapist), C. (2020, July 17). *How To Build An Interdependent Relationship With Your Partner?* Mom Junction. https://www.momjunction.com/articles/interdependence-in-a-relationship_00506789/

Judd, I. (2012, March 23). *Growing Together in Love.*

Huff Post. https://www.huffpost.com/entry/relationship-advice_b_1364078

Jacob, A., & Jacob, A. (2017, February 16). *4 steps to Building an Interdependent Marriage.* Nurturing Marriage. https://www.nurturingmarriage.org/routines-and-rituals/being-independently-dependent

Robbins, T. (n.d.). *6 Ways to Rekindle a Relationship.* Tony Robbins. Retrieved April 2, 2021, from https://www.tonyrobbins.com/love-relationships/5-ways-to-rekindle-a-relationship/

www.ingramcontent.com/pod-product-compliance
Lightning Source LLC
Chambersburg PA
CBHW022017290426
44109CB00015B/1203